SWAHILI - ENGLISH

POCKET DICTIONARY

JOSEPH SAFARI
HAMIS AKIDA

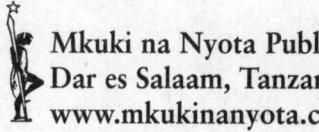

Mkuki na Nyota Publishers
Dar es Salaam, Tanzania
www.mkukinanyota.com

*First published by Mkuki na Nyota
Publishers, 6 Muhonda Street, Mission
Quarter, Kariakoo.
P.O. Box 4246, Dar es Salaam.
www.mkukinanyota.com*

First published in 2003

© J. Safari & H. Akida, 2003

ISBN 9976 973 79 9

Supplied by : Rainbow International
195, Jagriti Enclave, Delhi-110 092 India

Swahili/English Dictionary

This Swahili-English pocket dictionary follows up after the successful English-Swahili pocket dictionary. Although both dictionaries were originally conceived as aids to visitors to Tanzania and other Swahili speaking countries, the popularity of the first one with East African students proved its usefulness as a companion to Swahili speakers who are learning English. We are convinced that this Swahili-English pocket dictionary will also be as popular with the Swahili speakers learning English as it will be with foreign visitors to East Africa for whom it was originally planned.

The appeal of these pocket dictionaries lies mostly in their simplicity and straightforwardness. These qualities come from their authors who are renowned as being among the best Swahili language teachers and lexicographers with more than 30 years of teaching, research and other language related experiences.

The authors and publisher welcome comments, and ideas that would improve the Swahili-English Pocket Dictionary in its second and subsequent reprints.

Abbreviations:

adj.	Adjective
conj.	conjunction
adv.	adverb
interj.	interjection
n.	noun
v.	verb
pers.	personal
pron.	pronoun
ku	to as in to go, to see etc.
prep	preposition

Introduction to Swahili Pronounciation – part I

a	is always pronounced as in		f<u>a</u>ther
b	"	"	<u>b</u>o<u>b</u>, <u>b</u>it, <u>b</u>at
ch	"	"	<u>ch</u>eck, <u>ch</u>ess
d	"	"	<u>d</u>id, <u>d</u>octor
e	"	"	<u>e</u>lement
f	"	"	<u>f</u>ather, <u>f</u>eather
g	"	"	<u>g</u>o, <u>g</u>et
h	"	"	<u>h</u>ot, <u>h</u>ave
i	"	"	s<u>ee</u>, k<u>ee</u>p
j	"	"	<u>j</u>et, <u>j</u>ust
k	"	"	<u>k</u>ick
l	"	"	<u>l</u>ot
m	"	"	<u>m</u>other
n	"	"	<u>n</u>o, <u>n</u>u<u>n</u>
o	"	"	<u>o</u>.k. <u>o</u>ff
p	"	"	<u>p</u>ot, <u>p</u>ut
r	"	"	<u>r</u>un, <u>r</u>oot
s	"	"	<u>s</u>oft, <u>s</u>alt
t	"	"	<u>t</u>otal
u	"	"	p<u>u</u>t, <u>ou</u>t
v	"	"	<u>v</u>i<u>v</u>id, <u>v</u>ictor
w	"	"	<u>w</u>ater, <u>w</u>all
y	"	"	<u>y</u>es
z	"	"	<u>z</u>eal

The following typical Bantu words and sounds can only be learnt by listening carefully and practicing pronunciation after Swahili speakers. One need not be discouraged if one is unable.

To get it right after considerable effort. One should be encouraged by the knowledge that there are ethnic groups in East Africa who find the same difficulty in pronouncing those words. Some of the words are: mwana (child), mwenzi (friend), mwizi (thief), mwongo (liar), mganga (doctor), mgeni (visitor), mgongo (back), ng'ambo (across, the other side of a river, lake), ng'ang'ania (stick to, cling to), ng'ombe (cow), nyani (baboon), nyembe (razor blades), nyimbo (songs), nyinyi (you, second person plural), mpwa (nephew, niece), mpumbavu (fool), mpapai (papaya tree), mtwana (a person of lowly birth), mtumwa (slave), mtu (person), mtoto (child), mvua (rain), mvuke (steam, vapour), mvivu (lazy), etc.

The ng' sound as in ng'ang'ania is closest to the - ng - in (singing, hanging, or swinging).

Introduction to Swahili Pronunciation (part II), Morphology and Grammar

Swahili words are easy to pronounce, so much that a non Swahili speaker reading a Swahili text for the first time may make him/herself largely understood. That is not by any means to say that acquisition of the correct pronunciation is easy. On the contrary, one would need to spend a considerable stretch of time living and talking with good Swahili speakers to be able to acquire good diction. The following rules are a guide to Swahili pronunciation:

All consonants with the exception of G are pronounced as in English. G is pronounced as in "get", "go" and never as in "gin". F is pronounced as in "fire", "from", "field" and never as in "of". S is always pronounced as in "salt", "sail", "song" and never as in "visit" or "vision".

Some words have two consonants together followed by a vowel as in chakula, dhahabu, shamba and thelathini. Thus: CH is pronounced as in "child", "change", DH is pronounced as in "father", "fathom", SH is pronounced as in "shoe", "shirt"; and TH is pronounced as in "thin", "think".

Words with dh, th and gh sounds are of Arabic origin and present pronunciation difficulties for Bantu language speakers who would naturally pronounce them as z, s, and

g. examples are d̲h̲ana (concept), t̲h̲amani (value), g̲h̲ali (expensive).

Swahili has 5 vowels, a, e, i, o, u and each has one sound.

a is pronounced as a in "fast";
e is pronounced as e in "west";
i is pronounced as i in "see";
o is pronounced as o in "wall";
u is pronounced as u in "book".

When two vowels appear together, care must be taken to pronounce each one separately and distinctly, for the words with the two vowels have totally different meanings from those with one. For example: kufa (to die), kufaa (to be useful); paka (cat), pakaa (paint); kukata (to cut), kukataa (to refuse); and so on.

Swahili Morphology and Grammar

Since this dictionary is aimed at serving English speakers who have learned or are in the process of learning Swahili, the following summary of Swahili morphology and grammar may be found useful. Swahili morphology (the internal structure of Swahili words), is briefly described under the main headings; Pronouns and Pronominal Prefixes, Noun Classes, and Verbs. Many Swahili words are made up of roots and prefixes (or suffixes). Whereas roots do not change, prefixes many be changed. Hence for the same root, e.g. –tu, one may have m̲tu (a person, class 1), w̲atu (persons, class 2), k̲itu (a thing, class 7), v̲itu (things, class 8), j̲itu (a giant, class 5), and m̲ajitu (giants, class 6).

The following summary should be used for reference purposes since it is really very brief:

1. Pronouns and Pronominal Prefixes

1.1 Personal Pronouns

I: mimi; you (singular): wewe; he/she: yeye
We: sisi; you (plural): ninyi, nyinyi; they/them: wao/hao

1.2 Pronominal Prefixes

1.2.1 Subjects

Mimi <u>ni</u> naamka, <u>n</u>aamka (I am waking up, I wake up);
Wewe <u>u</u>naamka, <u>w</u>aamka (you are waking up, you wake up);
Yeye <u>a</u>naamka, aamka (he/she is waking up, he/she wakes up);
Sisi <u>tu</u>naamka, <u>tw</u>aamka (we are waking up, we wake up);
Ninyi <u>mn</u>aamka, <u>mw</u>aamka (you are waking up, you wake up);
Wao <u>wa</u>naamka, <u>wa</u>amka (they are waking up, they wake up).

1.2.2 Object

Mimi uta<u>ni</u>amsha (you will wake <u>me</u> up);
Yeye ata<u>ku</u>amsha (he/she will wake <u>you</u> up);
Mimi nita<u>mw</u>amsha, nita<u>m</u>piga (I will wake <u>him/her</u> up, I will beat <u>him/her</u>);
Wewe uta<u>tu</u>amsha (you will wake <u>us</u> up);
Sisi tuta<u>wa</u>amsheni (we will wake <u>you</u> up);
Mimi nita<u>wa</u>amsha (I will wake <u>them</u> up).

2. Noun Classes

Traditional grammar categorizes Swahili nouns into eighteen classes. These classes followed the Bantu languages class system which includes Swahili, as follows:

Class	Noun Prefix	Possessive Prefix	Demonstrative	Subject Prefix	Object Prefix
1	mu-(m-, mw-)	w-	huyu, huyo, yule	a-	-mu-(-m-mw-)

vii

2	wa-	wa-	hawa, hao, wale	wa-	-wa-
3	mu-(m-, mw-)	w-	huu, huo, ule	u-(w-)	-u-(-w-)
4	mi-	y-	hii, hiyo, ile	i-(y)	-i-(-y-)
5	ji, ø	l-	hili, hilo, lile	li-(l-)	-li-
6	ma-	y-	haya, hayo, yale	ya-	-ya-
7	ki-(ch-)	ch-	hiki, hicho, kile	ki-(ch-)	-ki-
8	vi-(vy-)	vy-	hivi, hivyo, vile	vi-(vy-)	-vi-
9	n-, ø	y-	hii, hiyo, ile	i-(y-)	-i-)
10	n-, ø	z-	hizi, hizo, zile	zi-(z-)	-zi-
11	u-	w-	huu, huo, ule	u-(w-)	-u-
12	nyu-	z-	hizi, hizo, zile	zi-(z-)	-zi-
13	u-(w-)	w	huu, huo, ule	u-(w-)	-u-
14	ma-	y-	haya, hayo, yale	ya-	-ya-
15	ku-(kw-)	kw-	huku, huko, kule	ku-(kw-)	-ku-
16	pa-	p-	hapa, hapo, pale	pa-(p-)	-pa- (definite)
17	ku-(kw-)	kw-	huku, huko, kule indefinite	ku-(kw-)	-ku-
18	mu-(mw-)		mw- humu, humo, mle mw-)	mu-(m-, mw-)	-mu-(m- mw-) (insideness)

On the list above, the class prefixes are shown in their singular and plural forms respectively. (Where there is the symbol "ø", it indicates that no prefix may be present.)

Other grammarians have contracted these classes to

eight in which singular and plural nouns that go together and use the same concordial prefixes make one class. The exceptions are in class five which combines both abstract and concrete nouns where concrete nouns take plural concordial prefixes and abstract nouns do not. However, classes five and six share the same concordial prefixes in their plural forms, the other exception is class eight which combines traditional forms. The other exception is class eight which combines traditional class sixteen, seventeen and eighteen as shown below.

	Class	*Examples*
1.	A-WA	mtoto <u>a</u>nalia
		watoto <u>wa</u>nalia
2.	U-I	mti <u>u</u>meanguka
		miti <u>i</u>meanguka
3.	KI-VI	kiti <u>ki</u>mevunjika
		viti <u>vi</u>mevunjika
4.	LI-YA	jiko <u>li</u>mechafuka
		majiko <u>ya</u>mechafuka
5.	U-(ZI)	ugonjwa <u>u</u>meenea
		uzi <u>u</u>mekatika
		nyuzi <u>zi</u>mekatika
6.	I-ZI	nyumba <u>i</u>meungua
		nyumba <u>zi</u>meungua
7.	KU	kuimba <u>ku</u>zuri
8.	PA-MU-KU	nyumbani <u>pa</u>na kilio
		jikoni <u>m</u>(u) na panya
		mezani <u>ku</u>na chakula

3. Verbs

In the indicative or interrogative mood, the essential components of any finite verbs are: a subject prefix, a tense. Aspect marker, and a verb root, in that order. If an object prefix is inserted, this always precedes the verb root (see 1.2.2 above). When a verb is in the negative, a negation marker always precedes the subject prefix. The negation markers are /si-/, which replaces the pronominal subject prefix /ni-/, and /ha-/ before all the other subject prefixes.

3.1 Tense/Aspect markers

	Affirmative	Negative
present simple	-a-	-ø-
present continuous	-na-	-ø-
past simple	-li-	-ku-
future simple	-ta-	-ta-
perfective	-me-	-ja-
suppositional	-nge-	-singe-
conditional	-ki-	-sipo-
consequential	-ka-	-ku-
present habitual	hu-	-ø-

3.2 Verb suffixes/extensions

These occur after the root. When the verb root contains either of the vowels /a/, /i/ or /u/ the extension will contain the vowel /i/, and when the root contains either the vowel /e/ or /o/, the extension will contain the vowel /e/. The most common extensions are the following:

3.2.1 Applicative Extension: -i-, -e-

e.g. pitia (pass at), semea (speak for), katia (cut at/for), komea (stop at), shukia (descend at);

3.2.2 Causative Extension: -ish-, -esh-, -sh-, -z-

e.g. pitisha (make pass), semesha (make speak), katisha (cross, make out), komesha (force to stop), oza (make wed, marry);

3.2.3 Stative Extension: -ik-, -ek-, -lek-

e.g. pitika (be passable), semeka (be pronounceable), katika (be cuttable), oleka (be marriageable);

3.2.4 Passive Extension: -w-, -lew-

e.g. pitwa (be passed) semwa (be rebuked), katwa (becut), olewa (to be wed/married);

3.2.5 Reciprocal Extension: *-na-*
e.g. pita*na* (pass each other), sema*na* (rebuke each other), kata*na* (cut each other), oa*na* (marry each other).

For thorough instruction in Swahili grammar, the following three books are recommended:

Ashton E.O., *Swahili Grammar*, Longmans, U.K.
Safari J.F., *Swahili Made Easy*, Tanzania Publishing House, Dar es Salaam.
Wilson P.M., *Simplified Swahili*, Kenya Literature Bureau, Nairobi.

J. Safari
H. Akida

A

aa, ah, ahaa!, interj. expressing joy, pain, surprise, sudden discovery.

aalam, adj. the most knowledgeable (God).

abadani! adv. not at all.

abee! adv. response to a call made by women, for men it is **naam!**

abiria, n. passenger, *gari la abiria*, passengers car, *meli ya abiria*, passenger ship, or boat.

abjadi, n. alphabet.

abu, n. father.

abudu, ku-, v.t. to worship, *abudu Mungu*, worship God.

abunusi, n. ebony tree.

acha, ku-, v.t. to leave, stop doing, *acha upuuzi*, stop your nonsense 2. abandon, *acha shule*, stop going to school, *amemwacha mke wake*, he has left his wife.

achama, ku-, v.i. to gape, open the mouth wide.

achana, ku-, v.t. to part company, separate, *wameachana*, they have separated from each other, *achana naye*, leave him alone, do not associate with him.

achanisha, ku-, v.t. cause to separate, uncouple.

achia, ku-, v.t. to let go, *achia kamba*, let go of the rope.

achika, ku-, v.i. to be divorced, *Asha ameachika*, Asha has been divorced.

achilia, ku-, v.t. let go (see **achia**), *achilia mbali hayo*, leave that alone.

achisha, ku-, v.t. cause to stop, *achisha kazi*, fire a worker, *je, ameacha kazi au ameachishwa?* did he resign or was he sacked from his job?

achwa, ku-, v.t. be divorced, be abandoned.

ada, n. fee, *ada ya shule*, school fee 2.(sl) *kama*

ada, as usual.
adabu, n. behaviour, politeness, *adabu njema*, good behaviour, etiquette, *hana adabu*, he is bad mannered.
adhabu, n. penalty, punishment, *kutoa adhabu*, to punish, *kupata adhabu*, to be punished.
adhama, n. greatness, honour, glory.
adhibu, ku-, v.t. to punish, afflict.
adhimisha, ku-, v.i. to celebrate.
adhini, ku-, v.t. call Moslems to community prayer.
adhiri, ku-, v.t. put someone to shame.
adhirika, ku-, v.t. be put to shame.
adhuhuri, n. period between noon and 2 pm.
adili, ma, n. ethical conduct, moral conduct, ethics.
adilisha, v.t. edify, moralize.
adimika, ku-, v.i. be scarce, *sukari imeadimika*, sugar is scarce.
adimu, adj. scarce, unobtainable easily.
adrenalini, n. adrenalin.
adui, ma, n. enemy, foe, *maadui zetu*, our enemies.
advansi, n. advance.
afa, ma, n. disaster, calamity.
afadhali, adv. much better.
afiki, ku-, v.i. to agree, come to terms with somebody, *naafiki hayo*, I agree with that.
afikiana, ku-, v.t. agree with one another, come to compromise.
Afrika, n. Africa.
Afrikanaizesheni, n. Africanization.
afueni, n. recovery from illness.
afya, n. health, *ana afya nzuri*, he is healthy, *hana afya nzuri*, he is not healthy.
aga, ku-, v.t. to take leave of, to say good-bye, *mbona hamkuniaga?* why didn't you say goodbye to me?

agana, ku-, v.t. to promise to each other 2. to take leave of one another, to say goodbye to one another.

agano, ma-, n. promise, covenant, *Agano Jipya,* New Testament, *Agano la Kale,* Old testament.

aghalabu, adv. as a rule, more often.

agiza, ku-, v.t. to order for something, *ameagiza vitabu,* he has put in an order for books.

agizia, ku-, v.t. order for sth on behalf, give instructions to do sth on behalf.

agizo, ma-, n. order, instruction(s), command(s), *ametoa agizo,* he has given an order.

Agosti, n. August.

agronomia, n. agronomy.

agua, ku-, v.t. to prophecise 2. treat medically, to interpret dreams.

ahadi, n. promise, *toa ahadi,* make a promise, *ahadi ni deni,* a promise is a debt.

ahera, n. the next world, life after death, *tutaonana ahera,* we shall meet in the next world.

aheri! n. *aheri yako!,* good for you!

ahidi, ku-, v.i. to promise, *ameahidi,* he has promised.

ahirisha, ku-, v.t. adjourn, postpone, shunt.

ahueni, n. better condition (health), *nina ahueni,* I feel better.

aibika, ku-, v.i. to be disgraced.

aibisha, ku-, v.t. put to shame, disgrace, dishonour.

aibishana, ku-, v.t. put one another to shame.

aibishwa, ku-, v.t. dishonoured.

aibu, n. shame, disgrace, *pata aibu,* be disgraced, *tia aibu,* disgrace somebody.

aidha, conj. in addition to, futhermore, morover.

aina, n. sort, *aina gani?* what sort? *kila aina,* all sorts, type, kind.

aini, ainisha, ku-, v.t. to define, analyse.
aisee! adv. ghosh! look!
ajabisha, ku-, v.t. astonish, surprise.
ajabu, n. strange, *kiumbe wa ajabu*, a strange creature, wonder, *ni ajabu*, it is a wonder, *watu ni wengi ajabu!* there are so many people, it is a wonder.
ajali, n. accident, *ajali ya gari*, motor accident, car accident, *ajali haina kinga*, accident cannot be avoided (a Kiswahili saying).
ajili, n. reason, because of, for something, *kwa ajili yetu*, on our behalf.
ajira, n. employment, *hakuna ajira*, no vacancy.
ajiri, ku-, v.t. employ, hire people.
ajizi, n. negligence, slackness.
ajuza, ma-, n. very old woman.
aka! interj. expression of rejection, refusal, what? *aka!Sitaki*, what? I don't want.

akademia, n. academy.
akaunti, n. account.
ake, pers. pron. possessive, his, hers, it agrees with the noun, e.g. *nyumba yake*, his/her house, *wageni wake*, his or her visitors, guests.
akiba, n. savings, supply, reserve.
akida, ma-, n. headman, messenger.
akidi, n. marriage ceremony 2. quorum. 3. v.t. falsify, forge, complete.
akili, n. intelligence, reason, *mtoto huyu ana akili nyingi*, this child is very intelligent.
akiolojia, n. archaeology.
akisi, ku-, v.i. reflect, reverbarate.
ako, possessive pron. your (sing.), *mtoto wako*, your child, *watoto wako*, your children.
akronimi, n. acronymn.
akselereta, n. accelerator.
ala! alaa! interj. expression of amazement, really? *ala*,

alama   ambatana

ni kweli? really, is it true?
alama, n. (sing.) mark, *tia alama*, put a mark, indicate, sign.
alamsiki, adv. goodnight, goodbye.
alamu, n. alarm, warning signal.
alasiri, n. afternoon.
albino, n. albino.
aleluya, interj. alleluia.
alfa, n. alpha.
alfaalfa, n. alfalfa.
alfabeti, n. alphabet.
alfajiri, n. daybreak, dawn.
alhamdulilahi, n. praise be to Allah.
alhamisi, n. thursday.
alika, ku-, v.i. invite, *alika arusini*, invite to a wedding.
alikali, n. alkaline.
alimradi, conj. so long as, provided.
alizeti, n. sunflower.
alkemia, n. alchemy.
almasi, n. diamond(s).
altaneta, n. alternator.
altimeta, n. altimeter.
aluminiamu, n. aluminium.

alwatani, ma-, n. townsman, very famous person.
ama, conj. or, either, *ama kitabu hiki au kile*, either this book or that.
amana, n. pledge, a deposit, *weka amana*, give as a pledge.
amani, n. peace, *mazungumzo ya amani*, peace negotiations, *mapatano ya amani*, peace agreement.
amari, n. cable.
ambaa, ku-, v.i. pass by, *ambaa pwani*, walk along the coast (colloq.), go away, *wameambaa*, they have gone away.
ambacho, pron. which, that.
ambako, pron. where.
ambalo, pron. which, that.
ambamo, pron. where.
ambao, pron. whom, who.
ambapo, pron. where, *mahali ambapo ameketi*, where he sits.
ambatana na, ku-, v.i. stick to, *mtoto ameambatana na*

mamaye, the child is stuck to its mother.
ambatisha, ku-, v.t. fix on, attach, *ambatisha fomu hii na barua ya shule*, fix this form to the letter from school.
ambaye, pron. who, whom.
ambia, ku-, v.t. tell, *ameniambia yote*, he has told me everything.
ambilika, ku-, v.i. be advisable.
ambua, ku-, v.t. benefit from, *hana alichoambua*, he did not benefit at all.
ambukiza, ku-, v.t. to infect, *ugonjwa wa kuambukiza*, infectious disease, contaminate.
ambukizo, ma-, n. infection, contagion, *ugonjwa wa kuambukiza*, contagious diesease.
ameta, n. ammeter.
amfibia, n. amphibia.
ami, n. paternal uncle.
amia, ku-, v.t. chase off birds from the farm.
amiba, n. amoeba.

amina, interj. amen.
amini, ku-, v.t. trust, believe, *amini Mungu*, trust in God, *siamini*, I don't believe.
aminifu, adj. upright, trustworthy.
aminisha, ku-, v.t. aminisha, convince.
amiri, n. commander.
amka, ku-, v.i. wake up, get up.
amkia, ku-, v.t. greet, *je, tumekwisha amkiana?* have we greeted each other?
amonia, n. ammonia.
amplifaya, n. amplifier.
amri, n. order, *toa amri*, give an order, *fuata, shika amri*, obey an order, command.
amrisha, ku-, v.t. to order, give orders as in the military.
amsha, ku-, v.t. rouse from sleep, wake, arouse.
amua, ku-, v.t. settle a dispute, decide.
amuru, ku-, v.t. Command, *ametuamuru kukaa chini*, he has

commanded us to sit down.
amuzi, ma-, n. verdict, decision.
analojia, n. analogy.
anamometa, n. anemometer.
anasa, n. pleasure, easy life, luxury.
anatomia, n. anatomy.
andaa, ku-, v.t. prepare, make ready.
andalia, ku-, v.t. prepare something for somebody, *amewaandalia sherehe*, he has prepared a banquet for them.
andama, ku-, v.t. follow, *mwezi umeandama*, the new moon is out, *aliniandama mpaka jioni*, he followed me till evening, *mwandame mpaka akupe hela yako*, stick to him until he gives you your money.
andamana, ku-, v.i. walk together in a procession or demonstration.
andamizi, adj. senior, *afisa mwandamizi*, senior officer.
andazi, ma-, n. pastry, confectionery.

andika, ku-, v.t. write, to scribe.
andikia, ku-, v. write to, for, *ameniandikia barua nzuri*, he (she) has written me a nice letter.
andikiana, ku-, v.t. to correspond with each other, *andikiana*, write to one another or each other, *andikiana na*, to correspond with.
andikisha, ku-, v.t. register, *andikisha majina ya watoto*, have the children's names written down.
andiko, ma-, n. writing, scriptures.
anemia, n. anaemia.
anga, n. sky, atmosphere, *angani*, in the sky, *hali ya anga*, weather conditions.
angalau, conj. although, even though.
angalia, ku-, v.t. look at, be careful.
angalifu, adj. careful.
angamia, ku-, v.i. Perish, *mamia ya watu wameangamia kwenye tetemeko la ardhi*,

hundreds of people have perished in an earthquake.
angamiza, ku-, v.t. destroy, devastate.
angavu, adj. transparent, lucent, bright.
angaza, ku-, v.t. open one's eyes 2. shine, *mwezi umeangaza*, the moon is shining, *angaza macho*, stare.
angika, ku-, v.t. hang on a tree etc.
Anglikana, n. Anglican.
angu, poss.pron. my, mine.
angua, ku-, v.t. pluck, *angua nazi*, pick coconuts 2. hatch, *angua mayai*, hatch eggs, *angua kicheko*, burst out laughing, *angua kilio*, give a sudden, loud cry.
anguka, ku-, v.i. fall down.
anguko, ma-, n. fall, *maanguko(maporomoko) ya maji*, waterfall.
angusha, ku-, v.t. fell, bring down, knock down, *wapinzani wamemwangusha*, opponents have brought him down.
anika, ku-, v.t. put out to dry, *anika nguo*, hang clothes out to dry, to be aired.
ankra, n. invoice, bill of sale.
antena, n. antennae.
anthropolojia, n. anthropology.
antifona, n. antifon.
antiseptiki, n. antiseptic.
anua, ku-, v.t. take away from the sun, *asubuhi unaanika nguo na jioni unazianua*, you hang clothes in the morning, you take them away in the evening.
anuwai, adv. various.
anwani, n. address.
anza, ku-, v.i. begin, start, *anza kazi*, begin to work.
anzia, ku-, v.i. begin from, *anzia hapa*, begin from here.
anzisha, ku-, v.i. establish, *anzisha chama*, found a party.
ao, poss. pron. pl. their,

mali yao, their property, *watoto wao wanaumwa*, their children are sick.

apa, ku-, v.i. swear, *ninaapa*, I swear.

apisha, ku-, v.t. cause to swear, put on oath.

apiza, ku-, v.t. damn.

apizo, ma-, n. curse.

apostrofi, n. apostrophe.

Aprili, n. April.

ardhi, n. earth, piece of land, *nchi kavu*, dry land.

ari, n. zeal, *onyesha ari*, show some zeal, ardous.

arifiwa, ku-, v.t. be informed about sth.

arifu, ku-, v.t. inform, *mwarifu juu ya safari yako*, inform him/her about your journey.

arijojo, adv. go astray, miss the point/target.

arobaini, adj. forty, *nina umri wa miaka arobaini*, I am forty years old.

arusi, harusi, n. wedding, *bwana harusi*, bridegroom, *bibi harusi*, bride, *fanya arusi*, as a rule.

asali, n. honey, *fuata nyuki ule asali*, follow the bees to get honey.

asante, interj. thank you! *asante sana*, thank you very much.

asasi, n. beginning, essence of sth, institution, organisation.

asbesto, n. asbestos.

ashiki, n. passion for sth like desire for sex.

ashiria, ku-, v. signal, warn, presage, *hii inaashiria hatari*, this presages of danger.

asi, ku-, v.i. rebel 2. **maasi**, n. revolt, *askari wameasi*, soldiers have mutinied, *kuna maasi jeshini*, there is mutiny in the army.

asili, n. origin, source, nature, *asili yake nini?* what is its origin?

asisi, ku-, v.t. found, set up sth, *asisi chama cha siasa*, found a political party.

askari, ma-, n. soldier(s).

askofu, ma-, n. bishop(s), *askofu mkuu*, archbishop.

asteaste, adv. slowly, without hury.

asubuhi, n. morning, *habari za asubuhi*, good morning 2. in the morning.

atamia, ku-, v.t. brood, hatch eggs.

athari, n. defect, deficiency, effects, *athari za matumizi mabaya ya dawa*, the effects of drug abuse.

athiri, ku-, v.t. injure, affect negatively

ati! eti! interj. hey! (to attract attention) *eti ni kweli?* hey, is it true?

atlasi, n. atlas.

atomiki, n. atomic.

atomu, n. atom, *bomu la atomu*, atomic bomb.

au, conj. or *unakwenda sokoni au shuleni?* are you going to the market or to school?

aunsi, n. ounce.

awali, n. beginning (prov.), *awali ni awali, awali mbovu hapana*, take the first or nothing, *awali ya yote*, before all else.

awamu, n. phase, *serikali ya awamu ya tatu*, third phase government.

aya, n. verse, paragraph.

ayari, adj. disloyal, hypocrite.

azali, adj. eternal.

azima, ku-, v.t. lend, *niazimishe fedha*, please lend me some money 2. borrow, *je, naweza kuazima kalamu yako?* may I borrow your pen?

azimia, ku-, v.i. Intend, *tunaazimia kutembea kwa miguu*, we intend to walk on foot.

azimio, ma-, n. intention, determination, resolution 2. proposal, declaration, *Azimio la Arusha*, the Arusha Declaration.

azizi, adj. dear, *la azizi wangu*, my beloved 2. n. treasure.

azma, n. intention, purpose.

B

baa, ma-, n. calamity, disaster 2. bar, pub.
baada, prep. after.
baadaye, conj. later, after that.
baadhi, pron. some.
baba, n. father, *baba wa kufikia*, step father.
babaika, ku-, v.i. be confused, get startled.
babaisha, ku-, v.t. confuse sb, cause sb to be confused.
baba-krismasi, n. father christmas, Santa.
babatua, ku-, v.t. disfigure.
babu, n. grandfather.
bada, n. stiff porridge prepared from fermented cassava flour.
badala ya, prep. in stead of.
badhirifu, adj. extravagant.
badili, ku-, v.t. alter, substitute.
badilisha, ku-, v.t. exchange.

bafa, n. buffer.
baghami, n. idiot, foolish person.
bagua, ku-, v.t. discriminate.
bahameli, n. velvet.
bahari, n. sea, ocean, *Bahari ya Hindi*, the Indian Ocean.
baharia, n. sailor.
bahasha, n. envelope.
bahashishi, n. gratuity, tip.
bahati nasibu, n. lottery, a game of luck, bingo.
bahati, n. chance, *bahati nzuri*, good luck, *una bahati*, you are lucky, *bahati mbaya*, bad luck, misfortune.
bahatisha, ku-, v.i. guess, trust to luck, rely on luck.
bahili, adj. miserly, *huyu ni bahili mno*, he is so miserly, tight-fisted person.
baibui, n. garment worn by Moslem women on top of others.

baina, prep. between.

baini, ku-, v.t. to distinguish, discover the truth, *tumebaini ya kwamba u mpelelezi*, we have discovered that you are a spy.

bainifu, adj. evident, apparent.

bainika, ku-, v.i. to become clear, become well known, become transparent.

bainisha, ku-, v.t. make known, clarify.

bajeti, n. budget.

baka, ku-, v.t. rape 2. ma-, n. scar, spot(s).

baki, ku-, v.i. remain behind, be left over, stay behind, *alibaki nyuma*, he/she stayed behind.

bakia, ku-, v.i. stay behind, *hapakubakia kitu*, nothing was left over.

bakiza, ku-, v.t. leave something over, *hawakubakiza kitu*, they left nothing over.

bakora, n. walking stick, cane.

bakteria, n. bacteria.

bakuli, ma-, n. bowl, basin.

balaa, ma-, n. misfortune, *balaa gani hili*, what a misfortune! disaster see also **baa**.

balaghamu, n. sputum.

balasi, n. large jar for storing water.

balbu, n. balb.

balehe, ku-, v.i. to come of age.

bali, conj. but, *Juma hakwenda shule bali sokoni*, Juma didn't go to school but to the market.

balozi, ma-, n. ambassador.

balungi, n. grapefruit.

baluni, n. balloon.

bamba, ku-, v.t. arrest, catch, *amebambwa akiiba*, he was caught stealing.

bambam, adv. precisely.

bambatua, ku-, v.t. peel off, detach.

bamia, n. type of vegetable, okra.

bamiza, ku-, v.t. slam, bang.

bana, ku-, v.t. press,

banana

squeeze, pinch, *kubana matumizi*, to economise.
banana, ku-, v.t. be squeezed tightly together.
banda, ma-, hut, *anaishi kwenye banda lile*, he/she lives in that hut.
bandali, n. bundle.
bandama, n. (see **wengu**) spleen.
bandari, n. harbour, port, haven, *bandari ya salama*, haven of peace.
bandia, n. doll, make shift, fake, false, *nabii wa uongo*, false prophet, pseudo.
bandika, ku-, v.t. put something on something else, *kubandika dawa*, apply medicine on, *kubandika stempu*, affix a stamp, stick.
bandua, ku-, v.t. take something off, unstick.
banduka, ku-, v.i. be detached.
bangi, n. hashish, *vuta bangi*, smoke bhang, marijuana.
bangili, n. bracelet.
bango, ma-, n. poster,

baraka

placard, *mabango yamesambazwa kila mahali*, placards have been erected everywhere.
banika, ku-, v.t. roast.
banjo, n. banjo.
bano, ma-, n. pressure 2. bracket.
bantu, n. bantu.
banza, ku-, v.i. to press, *kujibanza pahali*, hide.
banzi, ma-, n. a splinter, chip.
bao, ma-, n. board, *piga bao*, fortune telling 2. score in sport, *wamepata bao moja*, they have scored, *tuliwafunga mabao matatu bila*, we scored three goals to nil.
bapa, ma-, n. flat surface 2. adj. flat.
bara, n. continent, mainland, *ninatoka Tanzania Bara*, I am from Tanzania Mainland.
barabara, n. road 2. adj. exactly
barafu, n. ice.
baragumu, ma-, n. horn blown to give alarm.
baraka, n. blessing, *hana*

barakoa   bawa

baraka, he has no blessing, *pata baraka*, be blessed, fortunate.
barakoa, n. mask, veil.
baraza, n. living room 2. council, *baraza la mawaziri*, cabinet, *Baraza la Usalama la Umoja wa*
barazahi, n. paradise.
baridi, n. cold, *vita baridi*, cold war.
bariki, ku-, v. consecrate, bless, *barikiwa*, be blessed.
barizi, ku-, v.i. chat with visitors leisurely, relax out of doors.
barua elektroni, n. an electronic mail, e-mail, *nimepokea barua-elektroni*, I've received an e-mail, also **barua-pepe**(common usage).
barua, n. letter, mail, *andika barua*, write a letter, *pokea barua*, receive a letter.
barubaru, ma-, n. teenager boy.
baruti, n. gunpowder, explosives, dynamite.
basha, ma-, n. sodomite, male homosexuel.
bashasha, n. charm, joy, 2. adj. jovial, social.
bashiri, ku-, v.i. also **tabiri**, fortune telling, predict, foretell.
basilika, n. basilica.
bastola, n. pistol, revolver.
bata, ma-, n. duck, *bata mzinga*, turkey.
bata-bukini, n. goose.
bata-mwitu, ma-, n. wild duck.
bati, ma-, n. tin, corrugated iron sheet, *tia nyumba mabati*, roof a house with bati.
batiki, n. batik.
batili, adj. invalid, null and void 2. n. annulment, invalid.
batilifu, see **batili**.
batilisha, ku-, v.t. cancel, annul.
batisfia, n. bathysphere.
batiza, ku-, v.t baptise, *John, ninakubatiza*, John, I baptise you
bavu, mbavu, n. rib, *mabavu*, force, *kwa mabavu*, by force.
bawa, ma-, n. wing of a bird.

14

bawaba, ma-, n. hinge.
bawabu, ma-, n. doorkeeper, porter.
baya, adj. bad, evil, *mtu mbaya,* a wicked person 2. adv. *vibaya,* badly, *anaumwa vibaya,* he is very sick 3. *mabaya,* evil things.
bayana, adj.adv. clear, obvious.
bayani, n. rhetoric.
bazazi, ma-, n. conman.
bazoka, n. bazooka.
beba, ku-, v.t. carry, take on the back, *beba mtoto,* carry a baby on the back.
beberu, ma-, n. a he-goat 2. imperialist.
bebesha, ku-, v.t. make somebody carry something.
bedui, ma-, n. nomad, bedouin, tramp.
bee! interj. yes (response by women).
bega, ma-, n. shoulder, *chukua kitu begani,* carry something on the shoulder, *bega kwa bega,* shoulder to shoulder.
begi, ma-, n. bag, sack, ruck sack.
behewa, ma-, n. railroad car, coach, carriage, *behewa la abiria,* passenger car.
bei, n. price, *bei gani?* how much? *pandisha bei,* raise the price, *punguza, shusha bei,* reduce the price.
beji, n. badge.
beki, ma-, n. defence (in football), *wana beki mbovu,* their defense is weak.
belele, bwelele, adv. excessively, abundantly.
beleshi, n. spade, shovel.
bembea, ku-, v.i. to swing.
bembeleza, ku-, v.t. to console, *bembeleza mtoto,* console a crying child, make it stop crying, fondle.
benchi, ma-, n. bench.
bendeji, n. bandage.
bendera, n. flag, *bendera ya taifa,* the national flag.
bendi, n. band.
benua, ku-, v.i. press so as to stick out.
bepari, ma-, n. capitalist.

beseni — binadamu

beseni, ma-, n. basin, tub.
besi, n. bass.
beti, n. stanza.
betri, n. battery, cell.
beua, ku-, v.t. despise, criticize.
beza, ku-, v.t. despise, lookdown on somebody or something.
bezo, ma-, n. scorn.
bi'kizee, vi-, n. very old woman.
bia, n. beer *kunywa bia*, drink some beer 2. **ubia,** n. share, take shares, share a business.
biarusi, n. bride.
biashara, n. business, trade, *biashara ya nje*, external trade, commerce.
bibi, n. grandmother 2. lady, memsahibu, girlfriend, *huyu ni bibi yangu*, this is my grandmother/girlfriend.
Biblia, n. Bible.
bibliografia, n. bibliography.
bibo, ma-, n. cashew apple.
bidhaa, n. goods, items, *wanaagiza bidhaa mbalimbali*, they order for different items, merchandise.
bidi, adv. be obliged to, be compelled.
bidii, n. effort, *fanya bidii*, make effort.
bidiisha, ku-, v.t. take special plans.
bikaboneti, n. bicarbonate.
bikari, n. compass, dividers.
bikini, n. bikini.
bikira, ma-, n. virgin, *ardhi isiyolimwa bado*, virgin land.
bikiri, ku-, v.t. defile.
bila, prep, without, nil.
bilahi, n. in God's name.
bilauri, n. tumbler, glass.
bili, n. bill.
biliadi, n. billiard.
bilioni, adj. billion.
bilulla, n. faucet.
bima, n. insurance, *unahitaji kuwa na bima ya maisha*, you need to have a life insurance.
bimkubwa, n. old woman.
binadamu, wanadamu, n. Adam's child, human being.

binafsi   bongo

binafsi, adv. private, privately, *mali binafsi*, private property.
binafsisha, ku-, v.t. privatise, *binafsisha mashirika ya umma*, privatise parastatal organisation.
binamu, ma-, n. cousin.
bingirisha, ku-, v.t. roll.
bingwa, ma-, n. champion, winner.
binti, ma-, n. daughter, *binti yangu ni mgonjwa*, my daughter is sick.
binua, ku-, v.t. protrude sth.
binya, ku-, v.t. squeeze, pinch, nip.
binzari, n. spice(s).
biogesi, n. biogas.
biokemia, n. biochemistry.
biolojia, n. biology.
bireta, n. biretta.
biriani, n. cooked rice mixed with fried steak and pepper.
birika, ma-, n. jug, kettle.
biringani, n. eggplant.
bisha, ku-, v.i. dispute, disagree, 2. knock at a door, *bisha hodi*, also *piga hodi*, knock at a door.
bisha, ku-, v.t. knock at the door 2. disobey, argue.
bisibisi, n. screwdriver.
boflo, (mkate) n. bread.
boga, ma-, n. pumpkin.
bohari, ma-, n. warehouse, store.
boksi, ma-, n. box.
bolti, n. bolt.
boma, ma-, n. fort, barricade, headquarter.
bomba, ma-, n. pipe, pump, tap, *bomba la maji*, water tap, *bomba la sindano*, syringe.
bombomu, n. sub-machine gun, bomb .
bomoa, ku-, v.t. demolish, dismantle, destroy.
bomoka, ku-, v.i. collapse, break down, fall in (house, etc.).
bonasi, n. bonus, premium.
bonde, ma-, n. valley, *bonde la ufa*, rift valley.
boneti, n. bonnet.
bonge, ma-, n. a big piece, *bonge la mtu*, giant, also **kibonge**.
bongo, n. brain, *tumia ubongo*, use your brain,

bonyea

bongoland, Tanzania, a country where one must use his brains in order to survive.

bonyea, ku-, v.i. give in under pressure, bend down under pressure.

bonyeza, ku-, v.t. press in, push a button, *bonyeza kengele*, ring a bell by pressing a button, give a click.

bora, adj. good, appropriate, best.

boresha, ku-, v.t. better, improve, *boresha kiwango cha maisha yako*, improve your life standard.

boribo, ma-, n. type of mango, big in size and reddish in colour.

boriti, ma-, n. post for roofing, the frame of the door or window.

boronga, ku-, v.t. mess up, muddle.

botania, n. botany.

bovu, adj. bad, rotten.

boya, ma-, n. buoy, raft.

braketi, n. bracket.

brandi, n. brandy.

brashi, n. brush.

buibui

buba, n. yaws.

bubu, ma-, n. dumb person, *kwa nini umekuwa bubu leo?* why are you so quiet today?

bubujika, ku-, v.i. bubble out, burst forth.

bubujiko, n. spring of water.

bucha, ma-, n. butchery.

buchari, n. large knife.

budi, n. choice, *sina budi*, I have no choice, I must, *yakubidi uende*, you must go, *hatuna budi kwenda*, we must go, have to.

bughudha, n. bother, disturbance.

bughudhi, ku-, v.t. bother, disturb, *usinibughudhi*, don't bother me, give trouble.

bugi, n. boogie.

bugia, ku-, v.i. swallow a big amount, gulp.

bugibugi, n. boogie-boogie.

buheri, adv. with happiness, with good health.

buhumu, n. lung.

buibui, n. spider, *utando wa buibui*, spider's web.

buki   busara

buki, n. kidney.
bukua, ku-, v.t. read intensively.
buldoza, ma-, n. bulldozer.
buluu, n. blue.
bumarengi, n. boomerang.
bumbuazi, n. perplexity, *shikwa na bumbuazi*, be completely taken aback, perplexed.
bumburuka, ku-, v. be startled.
bunda, ma-, n. heap, *bunda la vitabu*, a heap of books, a bundle of, *bunda la noti*, a bundle of bank notes.
bundi, n. owl, night bird.
bunduki, n. gun, *aliuwawa kwa bunduki*, he was shot dead, *piga bunduki*, shoot a gun.
bungala, n. thick sugarcane.
bunge, ma-, n. parliament, national assembly, *mbunge, wabunge*, member(s) of parliament.
buni, ku-, v.t. compose, guess, design, *buni mradi*, develop a project 2. n. coffee berry, coffee bean.
bunzi, ma-, n. maize cob.
buraa, n. forgivenss of obligation.
bure, adv. gratis 2. adj. useless, *hii ni kazi bure*, this is a useless work. 2. *alinipa kitabu bure*, he gave the book gratis to me, *amempiga mtoto bure*, he, she has beaten the child without reason.
buriani, n. bon voyage, farewell.
burudani, n. entertainment, amusement, recreation.
burudika, ku-, v.i. be refreshed, enjoy.
burudisha, ku-, v.t. entertain, refresh, recreate, *tutaburudisha wageni wetu*, we shall entertain our guests.
buruji, n. bugler.
burura, ku-, v.t. pull, drag, haul.
buruta, ku-, v.t. pull along, drag, haul.
busara, n. wisdom, *maneno ya busara*, words full of wisdom, prudence.

busha   chapa

busha, n. elephantiasis of the scrotum.
bushati, n. round bottom shirt.
bustani, n. garden.
busu, ku-, v.t. kiss, *nibusu*, kiss me 2. n. a kiss.
butaa, **butwaa**, n. amazement, *ameshikwa na butwaa*, he/she was amazed.
buti, ma-, n. boot (shoes/car).
butu, adj. blunt, *kisu butu*, blunt knife.
butwaa, n. perplexity, astonishment.
buyu, ki-, vi-, n. calabash.
bwa'mkubwa, n. old man.
bwabwaja, ku-, v.i. blab, jabber, talk nonsense.
bwaga, ku-, v.t. throw off, throw down.
bwalo, ma-, n. auditorium, hall.
bwana, ma-, n. lord, master 2. (colloq.) *twende bwana*, let us go friend, hello let's go (used by both men and women).

bwanashamba, ma-, n. agricultural officer.
bwanyenye, ma-, n. very rich person, bourgeois.
bwata, ku-, v.t. talk nonsense in a loud voice.
bwawa, ma-, n. dam, pool, pond, reservoir.
bwege, ma-, n. good for nothing, simpleton.
bweka, ku-, v.i. to bark, *mbwa huyu anatubwekea*, this dog is barking at us, bow-wow-wow..
bweni, ma-, n. hall of residence, dormitory.
bwerere, adv. abundance.
bweta, vi-, n. small box, compact.
bwete, adj. dormant.
bwia, ku-, v. to take-in in a large amount.
bwiko, n. arthritis.
bwimbwi, n. rice flour mixed with sugar and scraped coconut.
celebrate a wedding.

C

cha, ku-, v.i. to dawn, *kumekucha*, it is dawn.

cha, kucha, v.t. to feel reverend about, *kumcha Mungu*, to revere God, *mcha Mungu*, a person who fears God, who submits to God's will, 2. dawn, become daylight

chabanga, ku-, v.t. defeat an opponent.

chacha, ku-, v.i. rot, ferment, turn sour, turn bad, *chakula kimechacha*, the food has turned bad 2. fig. be upset, *baba amechacha*, father is very angry (upset), become bankrupty.

chachaga, ku-, v.t. wash clothes gently.

chachamaa, ku-, v.i. stand firm.

chachari, ma-, n. commonly used in the plural, *machachari*, excessive axcitement 2. resistance, *bwana huyu machachari sana*, this person is interestingly resistant, vigorous resistance.

chacharika, ku-, v.i. be restless.

chachawa, ku-, v.i. skip.

chache, adj. few in number, *siku chache*, a few days, *watu wachache*, a few people.

chachu, n. yeast, leaven, sour taste.

chachuka, ku-, v.i. become bad, ferment, go bad.

chafu, adj. dirty, *nguo chafu*, dirty clothes, *maneno machafu*, dirty words.

chafua, ku-, v.t. spoil, soil, dirten.

chafuka, v.i. become dirty (fig.), get angry, *bahari imechafuka*, the sea is stormy, the raging sea.

chafuko, ma-, n. confusion, chaos, absence of order, insecurity.

chafya, n. sneeze, *kupiga chafya*, to sneeze.

chaga, ku-, v.t. take up ones work or habit, with enthusiasm after some laxiness 2. begin a habit, *Polisi wa Usalama Barabarani wamechaga kukamata magari*, traffic police have begun to catch cars fast. 3. be prevalent, *homa ya malaria imechaga*, malaria has become rampant.

chagiza, ku-, v.i. insist, press a point.

chago, n. headboard.

chagua, ku-, v.t. choose, elect, *chagua kiongozi*, choose a leader 2. sift, *chagua mchele*, sift rice for cooking.

chaguo, n. choice.

chai, n. tea, *karibu chai*, welcome to a cup of tea.

chaji, ku-, v.t. charge.

chakaa, ku-, v.i. wear out, *shati lake limechakaa*, his shirt is worn out.

chakacha, n. coastal music that accompanies bell-dancing.

chakaramu, n. naughty person.

chakari, adv. very much, *walilewa chakari*, they were very drunk.

chakavu, adj. worn out, shabby.

chakaza, ku-, v.t. cause to wear out, make old.

chake, poss. pron. his/her/hers/ its.

chaki, n. chalk.

chako, poss. pron. your/yours.

chakubimbi, ma-, n. rumourmonger.

chakula, vyakula, n. food, *chakula kizuri sana*, very good food, *chakula bora*, nutritious food.

chakura, ku-, v.t. search by turning everything upside/down.

chale, n. cut(s), incision(s) made on the body by some peoples in Africa, Asia, South America etc.

chali, adv. on the back, *lala chali*, lie on one's back.

chama, vyama, n. club, party, *chama cha siasa*,

political party.
chamba, ku-, v.t. use water in place of toilet paper, *chamba mtoto*, wash the child after nature's call.
chambo, vy-, n. bait, anything used as bait, fish bait.
chambua, ku-, v.t. analyse, criticise 2. clean, sort out, *chambua pamba*, clean cotton by removing the seed(s).
championi, ma-, n. champion.
chana, ku-, v.t. comb, *chana nywele*, comb one's hair 2. to tear, *usichane karatasi*, don't tear that paper.
chanda, vy-, n. finger on which one wears wedding ring.
chandalua, vyandalua, chandarua, n. mosquito net(s).
chane, vy-, n. bunch of bananas/keys.
chang'aa, n. illicit spirits.
changa, adj. very young, *mtoto mchanga*, a baby 2. feel pains in the body especially in the muscles.
changa, ku-, v.t. collect, contribute something for a cause, *wanachanga fedha za shule*, they are collecting funds for a school, contribute, *changia harusi*, contribute for a wedding.
changamano, n. mixture, nearness.
changamfu, adj. cheerful, sociable.
changamka, ku-, v.i. be in good spirits, cheerful, *mbona umechangamka sana leo?* why are you so happy to day?
changamkia, ku-, v.t. to be enthusiastic about, *alituchangamkia sana*, he received us very cheerfully.
changamsha, ku-, v.t. cheer somebody up, instil good spirits, *changamsha darasa*, cheer up a class.
changanua, ku-, v.t. analyse.
changanya, ku-, v.t. mix, confound, blend, confuse,

changanyika   chea

unanichanganya, you confuse me.

changanyika, v.i. be mixed, *changanyikiwa*, be confused, mixed up.

changisha, ku-, v.t. collect contributions.

chango, n. small intestine, womb, hook.

changua, ku-, v.t. dismember.

changudoa, ma-, n. prostitute, harlot.

chanika, ku-, v.i. be torn.

chanikiwiti, n. green.

chanja, ku-, v.t. chop, *chanja kuni*, chop woods 2. to vaccinate.

chanjagaa, n. crab.

chanjo, n. incision, vaccination.

chanua, ku-, v.i. blossom.

chanya, n. positive.

chanyata, ku-, v.t. wash clothes gently.

chanzo, vy-, n. source, origin.

chapa, ku-, v.t. beat up, *alimchapa viboko*, he beat him/her with a stick several times, 2. **ku-**, v.t. print, *chapa vitabu*, print books.

chapaasili, n. archetype.

chapuza, ku-, v.i. haste.

chapwa, adv. unpalatable.

charaza, ku-, v.t. play a guitar, etc. 2. do with zest 3. strike, *alimcharaza fimbo*, he struck him/her with a stick.

charuka, ku-, v.i. become ferocious, *simba amecharuka siku hizi*, the lion has become ferocious nowadays, people are attacked often by a lion.

chasili, vya-, n. element.

chati, n. chart.

chatu, n. python.

chavua, n. pollen.

chawa, n. louse, lice, *kidole kimoja hakivunji chawa*, one finger does not kill a louse, i.e. unity is strength.

chea, ku-, v.i. fear, be apprehensive about, *mchea mwana kulia atalia mwenyewe*, he who fears the cry of his child will cry himself, spare the rod and spoil the child.

cheche — **cheua**

cheche, n. spark, *cheche la moto*, fire spark.
chechemea, ku-, v.i. limp.
cheichei, n. greeting used by children.
cheka, ku-, v.i. laugh 2. laugh at, *usinicheke*, don't laugh at me.
chekacheka, ku-, v.i. giggle.
chekea, ku-, v.t. smile at, *mtoto anakuchekea*, the baby is smiling at you.
chekecha, ku-, v. sift, i.e. in a sieve.
chekecheke, n. sieve.
chekelea, ku-, v.i. rejoice at.
chekesha, ku-, v.t. amuse.
cheko, n. laughter.
chelea, ku-, v.t. fear for.
chelewa, ku-, v.i. be late, *kwa nini umechelewa?* why are you late?
chelewesha, ku-, v.t. cause to be late, delay.
chema, adj. anything good.
chemba, vy-, n. seclusion, privacy.
chembe, n. grain, *hamna chembe*, nothing left.
chembechembe, n. cell.
chemchemi, n. water spring.
chemka, ku-, v.i. heat up, boil (of water).
chemsha, ku-, v.t. boil water on fire 2. miss a point.
chemshabongo, n. puzzle, crossword puzzle.
chenga, n. small bits, chips 2. act of dribbling, *piga chenga*, evade the other player by quick steps, dribble 3. dodge, *aliniona nikienda kwake, akanipiga chenga*; he saw me coming and he dodged me.
chenza, ma-, n. tangerine.
cheo, vy-, n. rank, status.
chepechepe, adj. wet, moist.
cherehani, vy-, n. sewing machine.
chereko, n. excitement.
chetezo, vy-, n. censer.
cheti, vy-, n. certificate, *cheti cha ualimu*, teacher's certificate.
cheua, ku-, v.i. belch.
cheua, ku-, v.i. chew the cud.

cheuo, ma-, n. cud.
cheza, ku-, v.i. play, *mtoto anacheza peke yake,* the child is playing all alone.
chezea, ku-, v.t. play with, *mpe mtoto kitu cha kuchezea,* give the child a toy to play with 2. mock, treat lightly, *acha kunichezea,* stop mocking me.
chezesha, ku-, v.t. cause to play, *chezesha mpira,* be a referee in a football game.
chezo, ma-, festivities, conjuring, illusory tricks, sorcery, *haya ni machezo,* said of an illness that is not easily treated (suspicion of witchcraft).
chezo, mi-, n. games, sports (see also **mchezo**).
chibuku, kibuku, n. brewed beer from cereals.
chicha, ma-, n. what remains of local brew when sifted through a sieve.
chifu, ma-, n. chief, headman.
chimba, ku-, v.t. dig, *chimba choo,* dig a latrine.
chimbia, ku-, v.t. bury.
chimbika, ku-, v.i. be deeply dug.
chimbo, ma-, n. mining place, mine quarry, *nafanya kazi machimboni,* I work in the mines.
chimbua, ku-, v.t. dig out, dig up.
chimbuko, ma-, n. source.
china, ku-, v.i. be stale.
chini, adv. on the ground, *lala chini,* lie on the ground, lie down.
chinja, ku-, v.t. slaughter by cutting the throat.
chinjana, ku-, v.t. kill one another.
chinjioni, ma-, n. slaughter house.
chinjo, ma-, n. act of slaughtering by cutting the throat, *anashitakiwa kwa kuua,* he is accused of manslaughter, murder.
chipsi, n. fried potatoes.
chipua, ku-, v.i. shoot up, *majani mapya yamechipua,* new leaves

have shot up.
chipubodi, n. chipboard.
chipukizi, ma-, n. young plant(s).
chipuko, ma-, n. shoot of plant.
chiriku, n. chatterer.
chizi, n. crazy person, 2. cheese.
chochea, ku-, v.t. poke at fire 2. stir up trouble, *chochea ghasia*, stir up a riot, evoke.
chochole, adj. poor, destitute.
chochote, adj. anything.
choka, ku-, v.i. get tired, *amechoka nawe*, he is tired of you.
chokaa, n. white plaster, *paka chokaa*, white wash a house.
chokesha, chokeza, ku-, v.t. see **chosha**.
chokoa, ku-, v.t. poke, pick at.
chokochoko, n. stirring trouble, aggression, acts intended to cause trouble, also **uchokozi**.
chokonoa, ku-, v.t. poke sth out.
chokora, ma-, n. street child.

chokoza, ku-, v.t. provoke sb, agress sb, tease sb.
chokoza, ku-, v.t. tease, vex, annoy.
chokozi, n. teasing, also **uchokozi**.
choma, ku-, v.t. pierce, stab, itch, burn, hurt psychologically, *choma moto*, set on fire 2. *choma kisu*, stab, *alimchoma kisu mpaka kufa*, he stabbed him to death.
chombeza, ku-, v.t. sooth, entice sb to give information.
chombo, vyombo, n. vessel, utensil, tool 2. ship, *vyombo vya angani*, space ships, equipment, instrument,
chomea, ku-, v.t. solder, burn into, weld sth.
chomeka, ku-, v.t. to pierce 2. to place into (of knife or spear).
chomekeza, ku-, v.t. stick something into.
chomelea, ku-, v.t. weld.
chomoa, ku-, v.t. take out, *chomoa kisu*, take a knife out.

chomoza   chubuka

chomoza, ku-, v.i. appear, *jua limechomoza*, the sun is out.
chonga, ku-, v.t. cut to shape, to sculpt.
chonganisha, ku-, v.t. set at odds.
chongea, ku-, v.t. cut to shape for somebody. 2. accuse, betray, *amewachongea kwa polisi*, he has betrayed them to the police.
chongesha, ku-, v.t. have something cut to shape, *chongesha mlango*, have a door made, *chongesha ufunguo*, make a duplicate key.
chongo, n. one-eyed person, *akipenda, chongo huona kengeza*, (love is blind (prov.)).
chongoka, ku-, v.i. be pointed 2. stick out.
chonjo, n. exaggeration, *tia chonjo*, exaggerate, *kaa chonjo*, be alert.
choo, vy-, n. toilet, water closet (w.c.).
chopea, ku-, v.i. limp, walk sideways.
chopoa, ku-, v.t. pull out

chopoka, ku-, v.i. slip out of hands.
chora, ku-, v.t. draw, *chora mbwa*, draw a dog.
choroko, n. green gram.
chosha, ku-, v.t. make tired, fed up.
chosha, ku-, v.t. tire, make one tired, tire somebody out.
chota, ku-, v.t. draw, *chota maji*, draw water, scoop.
chovya, ku-, v.t. dip into some liquid. *mchovya asali hachovyi mara moja tu* (prov.), he who dips his finger into honey, does not do it only once.
choyo, adj. miserly, stingy, greedy.
chozi, ma-, n. tear, *toa machozi*, shed tears, *tokwa na machozi*, have tears trickle down one's cheeks.
chuana, ku-, v.t. vie with one another in a sporting competition.
chubua, ku-, v.t. bruise.
chubuka, ku-, v.i. be bruised.

chubuko   chungua

chubuko, mi-, n. a bruise, *nina michubuko*, I have some bruises.
chuchu, n. nipples of breasts, teats.
chuchumaa, ku-, v.i. squat.
chuchumia, ku-, v.i. tiptoe.
chuja, ku-, v.t. filter, purify 2. select from 3. fade away.
chujuka, ku-, v.i. fade out in colour.
chuki, n. hatred, dislike, antipathy, *mauaji husababisha chuki ya kudumu*, killings cause permanent hatred.
chukia, ku-, v.t. hate, dislike, *nachukia uvutaji wa sigara*, I dislike smoking.
chukio, ma-, n. act of hatred.
chukiza, ku-, v.t. disgust, displease, embitter.
chukizo, ma-, n. abomination.
chuku, n. exaggeration, *piga chuku*, exaggerate.
chukua, ku-, v.t. take, *chukua mizigo*, take the loads, 2. take time, *safari itachukua wiki*, the trip will take a week, *chukua mimba*, become pregnant.
chukuana, ku-, v.t. resembe, be compatible.
chuma, ku-, v.t. pluck (fruit), 2. make profits, *chuma mali*, become rich, accumulate wealth.
chuma, vy-, n. iron, *chuma cha pua*, steel, *chuma maisha*, earn life 2. v.t. earn.
chumba, vy-, n. room, apartment.
chumvi, n. salt, *tia chumvi*, exaggerate, *kula chumvi nyingi*, live long.
chuna, ku-, v.t. skin a cow etc.
chunga, ku-, v.t. tend, *chunga mbuzi*, graze goats.
chungu, adj. bitter 2. disagreeable, painful.
chungu, vy-, n. cooking pot 2. heap, *vitu chungu nzima*, a lot of things.
chungua, chunguza, ku-, v.t. investigate, *polisi bado wanachunguza*, the

chungua   **chwa**

police are still investigating.
chungua, ku-, v.t. examine, inspect, inquire.
chungulia, ku-, v.t. look through a hole, give a quick look at something, peep, *angalia kwa haraka,* glance.
chungulia, ku-, v.t. peep at.
chunguza, ku-, v.t. examine, investigate.
chunguzi, adj. curious, investigative.
chungwa, ma-, n. orange.
chunusi, n. pimple.
chuo, vy-, n. college, *Chuo Kikuu,* university.
chupa, n. bottle 2. v. dive.

chupi, vy-, n. underpants, panties.
chupia, ku-, v.t. jump into.
chura, n. frog.
churupuka, ku-, v.i. slip from the hands, escape, *mwizi alichurupuka kutoka mikononi mwetu,* the thief slipped from our hands.
chururu, adv. watery.
churuzika, ku-, v.i. trickle down (liquids).
chutama, ku-, v.i. crouch.
chuuza, ku-, v.t. trade, sell retail.
chuya, n. unhusked rice in clean rice.
chwa, ku-; v.i. set (sun), *kumekuchwa,* the sun has set, become dusk.

D

da!, interj. expressing surprise, or sudden discovery.
dabwada, mi-, n. worn out clothes.
dada, n. sister, *huyu ni dada yangu*, this is my sister.
dadisi, ku-, v.t. inquire, investigate, spy on.
dafrao, n. head-on collision.
daftari, ma-, n. excercise book, copy book.
daftari, ma-, n. exercise book.
dafu, ma-, n. coconut full of milk.
dagaa, n. sardines.
dagaapapa, n. pilchard.
dahari, adv. ever, always.
dai, ku-, v.t. claim, demand 2. n. **ma-**, claim(s), *madai yako ni yapi?* what are your claims?
daima, adv. always, for ever.
dainamo, n. dynamo.
daka, ku-, v.t. catch in the air (ball etc.), *daka maneno*, interrupt, cut in on a conversation.
dakia, ku-, v.t. tiptoe, jump on to a vehicle, interject.
dakika, n. minute.
dakiza, ku-, v.t. interrupt conversation, *dakiza maneno*, interrupt people's conversation.
dakizo, n. interruption, interjection.
daktari, ma-, n. doctor (medical), *daktari wa tiba*.
daku, n. last meal before dawn.
daladala, n. commuter buses, shuttle buses.
dalali, ma-, n. auctioneer, middleman in business, broker.
dalili, n. sign, symptoms, *dalili za homa*, symptoms of fever.
daluga, n. spikes.
damka, ku-, v.i. get up

31

dampo — deka

very early in the morning.
dampo, ma-, n. dumping place.
damu ya mzee, n. maroon.
damu, n. blood, *anatoka damu*, he/she is bleeding, *damu itamwagika*, there will be violent incidents, blood will be spilled.
danadana, n. dribbing.
dandia, ku-, v.t. scramble into, stow away.
danganya, ku-, v.t. cheat, tell lies, deceive.
danganyifu, adj. deceitful.
danganyifu, adj. false, deceitful, insincere.
danganyika, ku-, v.i. be deceived, *umedanganyika*, you have been deceived.
danguro, ma-, n. brothel.
dansi, n. dance.
daraja, ma-, n. level, stage, bridge, *jenga daraja*, build a bridge.
daraka, ma-, n. responsibility, authority.
darasa, ma-, n. class room, class, *mtoto wa Darasa la Kwanza*, a child following class one.

darizi, ku-, v.t. practise embroidery, 2. n. embroidery.
darubini, n. telescope, microscope.
dasta, n. duster.
data, n. data.
dau, n. an amount of money put down for gambling 2. n. a dhow for sailing across the river or for fishing along the sea, *mdau*, beneficiary, stake holder.
dawa, n. medicine, *pata dawa*, get medicine, *dawa ya kuhara*, purgative.
dawati, ma-, n. desk.
dayosisi, n. diocese.
dazeni, n. dozen.
debe, ma-, n. a tin, can, *debe la maji*, a tin full of water.
dede, adv. unsteady just like a child learning to stand up and walk.
degedege, n. an attack of acute malaria, convulsions.
deka, ku-, v.i. to be spoiled, *mtoto huyu anadeka*, this child is spoiled.

dekeza   dharau

dekeza, ku-, v.i. spoil a child.
deki, ku-, v.t. mop the floor.
dekua, ku-, v.i. bring down with one shot.
delta, n. delta.
demadema, n. toddle.
demokrasia, n. democracy.
demu, n. dame, girlfriend.
denda, n. drool, spittle.
dengua, ku-, v.i. show off.
deni, ma-, n. debt, *dai deni*, claim a debt, *lipa deni*, pay a debt.
depo, ma-, n. depot, warehouse, *depo la serikali*, government depot.
dereli, n. drill, *piga dereli*, do drilling.
desimali, n. decimal.
desturi, n. custom, habit, also **dasturi**.
deuli, n. pall, cloth for holding a sword to the waist.
dhabihu, n. sacrifice.
dhahabu, n. gold, *mkufu wa dhahabu*, golden chain.
dhahiri, adj. clear, evident, apparent, *ni dhahiri*, it is evident, clear, distinct.
dhaifu, adj. weak, powerless, helpless, decrepit.
dhalili, n. wretch.
dhalimu, n. oppressive, tyranny.
dhamana, n. bond, bail, *wekea mtu dhamana*, give somebody surety.
dhambi, n. sin, crime, *utoaji mimba ni dhambi*, abortion is a sin.
dhambi, n. sin, offence, fall.
dhamini, ku-, v.t. give bail to somebody, sponsor somebody.
dhamira, n. subject matter, intention.
dhamiri, n. conscience, *dhamiri inayoshitaki*, a guilty conscience.
dhamiria, ku-, v.i. to intend.
dhana, n. concept, idea, mentality, conjecture.
dhani, ku-, v.i. think, surmise.
dhania, ku-, v.t. suspect.
dharau, ku-, v.t. despise, contempt, look down, *usidharau wengine*,

don't look down on others.
dhariri, n. radiation dust.
dharuba, n. sudden calamity.
dharura, n. emergency, *mkutano wa dharura*, an emergency meeting.
dhati, n. purpose, *kwa dhati*, in a determined way.
dhibiti, ku-, v.t. control, sensor.
dhifa, n. banquet.
dhihaka, n. ridicule, mockery, *kumdhihaki mtu*, to ridicule somebody.
dhihaki, ku-, v.t. mock, ridicule.
dhiki, n. want, distress.
dhikiri, ku-, v.t. mention the name of Allah (Moslems).
dhima, n. duty, responsibility, obligation, liability.
dhoofika, dhoofu, ku-, v.i. become weak.
dhoofisha, ku-, v.t. to weaken, *UKIMWI umemdhoofisha*, AIDS has weakened him.

dhoofu, adj. weakened, of bad health.
dhoruba, n. rainstorm.
dhuluma, n. unjust treatment, fraud, injustice.
dhulumu, ku-, v.t. treat unjustly, defraud.
dhuria, n. descendants.
dhuru, ku-, v.t. harm, injure.
dibaji, n. preface, foreword.
didimia, ku-, v.i. sink, lose in business.
didimiza, ku-, v.t. submerge, cause to sink.
difensi, n. defence.
difu, n. differential.
digrii, n. degree.
dikteta, ma-, n. dictator, *mauaji ya dikteta*, the assassination of a dictator.
dimba, n. farrow bush 2. n. round, *fungua dimba*, opening round (first round).
dimbwi, ma-, n. pool.
dinari, n. dinar.
dinda, ku-, v.i. stand firm, erect (penis).
dini, n. religion, *dini ya*

dinosau   dondoo

asili, traditional religion.
dinosau, n. dinosaur.
diploma, n. diploma.
dira, n. compass, *fuata dira,* follow the compass direction.
diriki, ku-, v.i. be able to, *sikudiriki,* I did not chance to do it.
dirisha, ma-, n. window.
disa, ku-, v.i. be erect (penis).
dishi, n. dish, food.
diskaunti, n. discount.
dispensari, n. dispensary.
divai, n. wine.
divisheni, n. division.
diwani, ma-, n. councillor.
dizeli, n. diesel.
do! interj. damn!
doa, ma-, n. stain, spot, *madoadoa,* spotted.
dobi, ma-, n. laundryman.
doda, ku-, v.i. go stale/ bad.
dodo, n. type of mango that becomes quite big and remains green when ripe.
dodoki, ma-, n. loofah fruit.
dodosa, ku-, v.t. drawl, cross examine, interview.
doea, ku-, v.t. try to get a free meal, sponge on somebody.
dogo, adj. small, little, *baba mdogo,* a younger brother to one's father.
dogodogo, adj. petty, piddling.
dogori, ma-, n. exorcising dance.
dokeza, ku-, v.t. give a hint.
dokoa, ku-, v.t. pilfer, steal small amounts.
dola, ma-, n. state, empire, *Nchi za Jumuiya ya Madola,* Common Wealth States.
dole, n. a single banana/ finger.
domo, ma-, n. big mouth.
domokaya, n. blabber, chatterbox.
dona, n. maize flour.
donda, ma-, n. wound, ulcer, *dondandugu,* an ulcer which does not heal.
dondoa, ku-, v.t. pick one at a time like grains.
dondoka, ku-, v.i. fall down, drip.
dondoo, n. excerpt,

promiscuity, steinbuck.
donge, ma-, n. lump.
donoa, ku-, v.i. pick at as a bird 2. pilfer.
doria, n. patrol, *polisi wa doria*, the patrol police.
dosari, n. blemish, defect, short-coming.
doti, n. a pair, *doti ya kanga*, two pieces of kanga cloth, a pair.
dragoni, n. dragon.
drama, n. drama.
drili, n. drill.
dua, n. prayer.
duara, n. circle.
dubu, n. a bear.
dubwana, ma-, n. a giant creature.
dude, ma-, n. object of vague quality, *dude gani hili*? What is this? What a monster!
dudu, ma-, n. big insect.
dudumizi, n. whitebrowed coucal.
dugi, adj. blunt.
duka, ma-, shop, *anzisha duka*, open a shop.
dukuduku, n. grudge, doubt.
duma, n. cheetah.
dumaa, ku-, v.i. fail to grow to normal size, be stunted, fail to develop fully.
dumaza, ku-, v.t. stunt, inhibit.
dumbukiza, ku-, v.t. drop something into.
dume, ma-, n. male animal.
dumisha, ku-, v.t. perpetuate.
dumu, ma-, n. pot, container of water usually made of copper or silver, or nylon, 2. ku-, v.i. last long.
dumuzi, n. corn borer.
dunda, ku-, v.i. bounce on the ground, e.g. *dunda mpira*, throw the ball on the ground several times.
dunduliza, ku-, v.i. save up little by little.
dunga, ku-, v.t. inject with, bore, *dunga sindano*, give an injection.
dungu, n. watchtower, tribune.
duni, adj. of low quality, *hali duni*, poor condition.
dunia, n. the earth, *sayari*

dunisha

ya dunia, planet earth, the world.
dunisha, ku-, v.t. debase, make inferior.
duru, n. turn, round.
durusu, ku-, v.t. study a book, read with concentration.

duzi

duwaa, ku-, v.i. be taken aback.
duwaza, ku-, v.t. non plus, stagger.
duwazi, ma-, n. arthralgia.
duzi, wa-, n. gossip-monger, slanderer.

E

ebo! interj. expression of contempt.

ebu, inter. call somebody to attention, well, *ebu nione*, let me see, come then, *ebu njoo*, please come.

eda, n. period when a woman remains unmarried and under care of husband's relatives after divorce or husband's death.

ee! interj. O! *ee! Mungu*, O! God.

egama, ku-, v.t. depend on, be close sth.

egemea, ku-, v.t. lean, rely on, *egemea ukuta*, lean on the wall, *egemea*, rest on, lean on.

egemeo, ma-, n. support, pivot, fulcrum.

egemeza, ku-, v.t. repose, support.

egesha, ku-, v.t. park a car, put against a wall etc.

egesho, ma-, n. parking, parking lot.

ehee! interj. that's it! okay!

ehee! interj. yes, okay, aha!

eka, n. acre.

ekaristi, n. Eucharist.

ekseli, n. axle.

eksirei, n. X-ray.

ekumeni, n. ecuminism.

ekundu, adj. red, reddish.

ekzosi, n. exhaust.

elea, ku-, v.i. float, *elea angani*, float in the sky, be afloat, swim.

eleka, ku-, v.t. carry astride on the hip.

elekea, ku-, v.i. point to, appear to be, going in a definite direction, *ndege inaelekea kusini*, the plane is heading to the south.

elekevu, adj. bright.

elekeza, v.t. direct, show the way to, instruct.

elekromita, n. electrometer.

elektroni, electron.

elemea, v.t. oppress, weigh heavily upon.

elemewa   enye

elemewa, ku-, v.t. be overwhelmed, be too much occupied.
eleveta, n. elevator.
elewa, v.i. understand, *elewa nikwambiayo*, understand what I tell you.
eleza, v.t. explain, expound.
elezea, ku-, v.t. narrate.
elfu, adj. thousand, *shilingi elfu moja*, one thousand shillings.
elimisha, v.t. educate, teach, enlighten, *elimisha vijana juu ya UKIMWI*, educate the youth on AIDS.
elimu, n. education, knowledge.
elimudunia, n. cosmology.
elimukifungo, n. penology.
elimumaadili, n. ethics.
elimumimea, n. botany.
elimumsamiati, n. lexicology.
elimumwendo, n. dynamics.
elimusiha, n. hygiene.
elimuujuzi, n. epistemology.
elimuwadudu, n. pestology.

ema, adj. kind, good.
embamba, adj. slim, thin, narrow, *njia nyembamba*, a narrow path.
embe, ma-, n. mango.
enda, ku-, v.i. go, *unaenda wapi?* Where are you going?
enda-kombo, ku-, v.i. deviate.
endea, ku-, v.t. go for, go towards.
endekeza, ku-, v.t. treat leniently, spoil.
endelea, ku-, v.i. progress, develop.
endeleza, ku-, v.t. cause to develop.
endesha, ku-, v.i. drive, to lead, to head, to run, *endesha biashara*, run business.
enea, ku-, v.i. spread, abound.
eneo, ma-, n. area.
eneza, ku-, v.t. extend over.
engua, ku-, v.t. skim, take scum off water/milk.
enu, adj. pron. your, yours (pl.).
enye, adj. possessing, *mtu*

enyewe

mwenye mali, a rich person.
enyewe, pron. self, actual.
enzi, n. power, in the rule of, *enzi za utawala wa Nyerere*, in the rule of Nyerere.
epa, ku-, v.t. avoid.
epesi, adj. light.
epifania, n. Epiphany.
epistemolojia, n. epistemology.
epsiloni, n. epslon.
epua, ku-, v.t. take off, remove.
epuka, ku-, v.t. avoid, *epuka makundi mabaya*, avoid bad company.
epuka, ku-, v.t. avoid, escape.
epukana, ku-, v.t. shun.
epusha, ku-, v.t keep away from, help somebody to avoid something.
erevu, adj. clever.
erevuka, ku-, v.i. become clever, become knowledgeable.
erevusha, ku-, v.t. prime.
eropleni, n. aeroplane.
esperanto, n. esperanto.
ethili, n. ethyl.
ethnolojia, n. ethnology.
etimolojia, n. etymology.
eupe, adj. white, *moyo mweupe*, clean heart, without a grudge.
eusi, adj. black.
eutenasia, n. euthenasia.
ewe! interj. you there!
ezeka, ku-, v.t. thatch, *ezeka nyumba*, roof a house, *nyumba iliyoezekwa kwa nyasi*, a grass thatched house.
ezi, n. power, *Mwenyezi Mungu*, Almighty God.
ezua, ku-, v.t. remove a roof, *upepo umeezua paa la shule*, the wind has removed the roof of the school building.

F

fa, ku-, v.i. die, perish, benumbed.
faa, ku-, v.i. be of use, fit a purpose.
fadhaa, fazaa, n. confusion, depression, *shikwa na fadhaa,* become confused.
fadhaika, ku-, v.i. be confused, be depressed.
fadhaisha, ku-, v.i. confuse, disappointing.
fadhila, n. kindness, favour, *umenifanyia fadhila kubwa,* you have done me a great favour.
fadhili, n. kindness, favour 2. **ku-,** v.t. sponsor somebody or something.
fafanua, ku-, v.t. explain clearly, clarify, ellaborate, *fafanua hoja zako,* clarify your point.
fagia, ku-, v.t. sweep.
fagio, ma-, n. broom, brush.
fagositi, n. phagocyte.
fahali, ma-, n. bull, *mafahali wawili hawakai zizi moja,* two bulls cannot stay in the same kraal(shed).
fahamiana, ku-, v.t. know each other.
fahamika, ku-, v.i. be well known.
fahamika, ku-, v.t. be known, be famous.
fahamisha, ku-, v.t. inform, instruct, introduce.
fahamisha, ku-, v.t. inform.
fahamu, ku-, v.t. understand, acquainted, know, *je, unafahamu kwamba...,* do you know that...
fahamu, n. senses.
faharasa, n. table of contents.
fahari, n. glory, pomp, pride.
faida, n. profit, *faida halisi,* net profit.
faidi, ku-, v.i. profit from.
faidika, ku-, v.i. prosper, profit from, benefit from.

faili   **fariji**

faili, ma-, n. file (of papers), folders.
fainali, n. final game.
faini, n. fine, penalty, *toza faini*, fine.
faini, n. fine.
falsafa, n. philosophy, *elimu ya hekima*, science of wisdom.
fana, ku-, v.i. prosper, succeed.
fanaka, n. prosperity, success.
fanana, ku-, v.i. look alike.
fanana, ku-, v.t. be similar, resemble.
fananisha, ku-, v.t. compare, mistake one person for another.
faneli, n. funnel.
fani, n. area of study, *Kitivo cha Fani na Elimu-Jamii*, Faculty of Arts and Social Sciences.
fanicha, fenicha, n. furniture.
fanikio, ma-, n. success.
fanikisha, ku-, v.t. accomplish.
fanikiwa, ku-, v.t. succeed, prosper.
fanusi, n. kerosene lamp.

fanya, ku-, v.t. do, make, *fanya kazi*, work, *fanya biashara*, carry on trade, *fanya bidii*, exert oneself, *fanya kelele*, make noise; *fanya matata*, make trouble; *fanya fujo*, make trouble; *fanya haraka*, make haste; *fanya shauri*, consult each other; *fanya mkataba*, enter into contract; *fanya mzaha*, make fun of; *fanya safari*, travel; *fanya udhia*, cause nuisance.
fanyia, ku-, v.t. do sth for sb.
fanyika, ku-, v.i. be done.
faragha, n. privacy, *kwa faragha*, privately.
faraja, n. consolation, *pata faraja*, be consoled.
farakana, ku-, v.i. differ in opinion.
farakano, ma-, division, misunderstanding.
farakisha, ku-, v.t. alienate.
farasi, n. horse, *panda farasi*, ride a horse.
fariji, ku-, v.t. console,

fariji wagonjwa, console the sick, comfort.

fariki, ku-, v.i - **dunia**, die (said of people).

farishi, ku-, v.t. make a bed.

faru, n. also **kifaru**, rhinoceros. 2. military tank.

fasaha, adj. correct (style), fluent, *Kiswahili fasaha*, correct Swahili usage.

fasheni, n. fashion.

fashisti, ma-, n. fascist.

fasihi, n. literature, *fasihi simulizi*, oral literature.

fasili, ku-, v.t. define, annotate.

fasiri, ku-, v.t. translate, interpret, *fasiri maandiko*, interpret the writing, text, construe.

fataki, n. explosive device, dynamite.

fauka, adv. besides, apart from that.

faulu, ku-, v.i. succeed, pass examination.

Februari, n. February.

fedha, n. money, currency, *fedha za kigeni*, foreign currency (exchange).

fedheha, n. shame, disgrace.

fedhehesha, ku-, v.t. abash.

fedhuli, n. insolent person, rude.

feki, n. fake.

feli, ku-, v.t. fail, *feli mtihani*, fail an examination.

fenesi, n. jack-fruit.

feni, n. fan.

feruzi, n. sky-blue.

fia, ku-, v.i. die for, at, *amefia njiani*, he died on the way (to hospital etc.).

ficha, ku-, v.t. hide, keep secret.

fichama, ku-, v.i. be hidden, lie low.

ficho, ma-, n. hiding place.

fichua, ku-, v.t. uncover, make public.

fichuo, ma-, n. discovery, revelation.

fidhuli, see **fedhuli**.

fidia, n. compensation, reparation, ransom, - v.i. pay ransom.

fidla, n. fiddle, violin.

fifia, ku-, v.i. fade, wither, *rangi imefifia*, the colour has faded away.

figa

figa, ma-, n. cooking stone.
figili, n. white radish.
figo, ma-, n. kidney.
fika, ku-, v.i. arrive, reach (a place, etc.).
fikia, ku-, v.i. arrive at, *mgeni amefikia kwao*, the guest has arrived at his/her home, *umefikia wapi mpaka sasa?* where have you reached so far?
fikicha, ku-, v.t. rub with hands, crumble.
fikira, n. thought, idea.
fikiri, ku-, v.i. think, have an opinion.
fikiri, ku-, v.i. think, ponder.
fikiria, ku-, v.i. think, consider, imagine.
fikirisha, ku-, v.t. preoccupy.
fikisha, ku-, v.t. convey.
fila, n. bad thing.
filamu, n. film.
filimbi, n. whistle, *piga filimbi*, blow the whistle.
filisi, ku-, v.t. confiscate, to liquidate in bankrupcy; *watoto wamemfilisi baba yao*, the children have made their
filolojia, n. philology.
fimbo, n. stick, *piga mtu fimbo*, to beat a person with a stick, cane.
fingirisha, ku-, v.t. make something roll along.
finya, ku-, v.t. pinch, *kiatu kinanifinya*, the shoe pinches me (too tight).
finyanga, ku-, v.t. make pottery, *finyanga matofali*, make bricks.
fira, ku-, v.t. practise sodomy 2. n. grey poisonous snake.
firaka, n. penis.
firauni, n. debauchee.
firigisi, n. gizzard (of birds).
firimbi, see **filimbi**.
fisadi, ma-, n. seducer, immoral person.
fisha, ku-, v.t. cause death, extinguish, discourage.
fisi, n. hyena.
fitina, n. mischief, intrigue, discord, *fanya fitina*, create discord.
fitini, ku-, v.t. create misunderstandings.
fito, n. pl. of **ufito**, a long

fiwa

pole used for building huts, etc.
fiwa, ku-, v.i. passive of fa, be bereaved, *amefiwa na baba yake*, his father has died.
fizikia, n. physics.
fiziolojia, n. physiology.
flamingo, n. flamingo.
flora, n. flora.
floraidi, n. floride.
florini, n. flourine.
fofofo, adv. completely, *lala fofofo*, sleep very soundly.
foka, ku-, v.i. run over (of water etc.) (fig.) bubble over 2. shout with anger.
fokasi, ku-, v.i. focus.
fokea, ku-, v.t. shout at, *usinifokee*, don't shout at me.
fomaika, n. formica.
fomu, n. form.
foni, n. phone.
fonimu, n. phoneme.
fora, n. victory, success in a performance, *tia fora*, excel.
forodha, n. custom house, *forodhani*, at custom's house.
forodhani, n. customs

fuatisha

house, port, harbour.
foronya, n. pillowcase.
foto, n. photograph, *fotoa*, 2. **ku-,** v.t. take a photo.
fotoa, ku-, v.t. take a photograph of sth.
fotostati, n. photostat.
fremu, n. frame.
frenolojia, n. phrenology.
friji, n. refridgerator, *friji mpya*, brand new refridgerator.
fu, adj. dead, **nyamafu,** meat from a dead, as opposed to slaughtered animal.
fua, ku-, v.t. hammer, *fua chuma*, forge iron 2. *fua nguo*, wash clothes 3. *fua nazi*, remove the shell of a coconut.
fuasa, ku-, v.t. also **fuata**, follow, *fuasa mfano*, imitate, model on somebody.
fuata, ku-, v.t. conform, follow.
fuatana, ku-, v.t. follow one another, go together.
fuatilia, ku-, v.t. follow up sth, pursue, investigate sth.
fuatisha, fuatiza, ku-, v.t.

fuawe — fumbo

fuawe, n. anvil (see **fua**).
fudifudi, adv. on the face, *lala fudifudi*, lie face down, also **kifudifudi**.
fudikiza, ku-, v.t. turn upside down.
fufua, ku-, v.t. raise from the dead, revive.
fufuka, ku-, v.i. rise from the dead, *Yesu Kristo amefufuka*, Jesus Christ has risen.
fufumka, ku-, v.i. sprout up.
fuga, ku-, v.t. keep domestic animals, tame 2. to grow, *fuga ndevu*, grow a beard.
fugo, mi-, n. domestic animals, cattle.
fuja, ku-, v.i. squander, *fuja mali*, spend carelessly.
fujo, n. disorder, chaos, *fanya fujo*, cause trouble, disorder, *kuna fujofujo*, confusion reigns.
fuka, ku-, v.i. *fuka moshi*, give off smoke.
fukara, n. poor.
fukia, ku-, v.t. bury something.
fukiza, ku-, v.t. fumigate.
fukua, ku-, v.t. dig out something.
fukusi, n. weavils.
fukuta, ku-, v.i. burn inwardly withouth flames being seen.
fukuza, ku-, v.t. chase, drive out, run after, *wanafukuza nini?* what are they chasing? *fukuza shule*, expel from school.
fulana, n. vest, flannel.
fulani, n. so-and-so.
fuliwa, ku-, v.i. have one's clothes washed; *nguo zimefuliwa*, clothes have been washed.
fuliza, ku-, v.i. do something without stop, also heard as **fululiza**.
fuma, ku-, v.t. weave cloth, *fuma nguo* 2. same as **fumania, ku-**, v.t find someone doing an immoral act, espy 3. low tide.
fumanizi, n. act of cat
fumba, ku-, v.t. close, *fumba macho*, close the eyes, use a veiled language.
fumbo, ma-, n. puzzle,

46

fumbua

enigma, mystery, *sema kwa fumbo*, use veiled language.
fumbua, ku-, v.t. open, disclose, *kufumba na kufumbua (macho)*, to open and close eyes, fast.
fumua, ku-, v.t. unstitch, uncover.
fumuka, ku-, v.i. come out, errupt, be unravelled.
funda, fundisha, ku-, v.t. teach, educate, teach morality, to impart moral education 3. n. mouthful.
fundi, ma-, n. skilled worker, technician, artisan.
fundisho, ma-, n. instruction, teaching, *mafundisho ya Kanisa*, the teachings of the Church, lesson.
fundo, ma-, n. knot.
funga, ku-, v.t. tie, close (door etc.), fast, abstain from eating, score a goal in a match.
fungamana, ku-, v.i. be in union with, *siasa ya fungamana*, policy of alignment.
fungamano, n. alliance, confederation.
fungana, ku-, v.t. score each other, be fastened together.
fungasha, ku-, v.t. collect one's goods and go.
fungate, n. honeymoon.
fungia, ku-, n. confine.
fungu, ma-, n. heap, share.

funza

fungua, ku-, v.t. open, *fungua mlango*, open the door.
funguka, ku-, v.i. break open, break loose.
fungulia, ku-, v.t. open for, release, let out.
funguo, pl. of **ufunguo**, key.
fungutenzi, ma-, n. verb phrase.
funika, ku-, v.t. cover, put a lid on; *kujifunika*, to cover oneself.
funua, ku-, v.t. unveil, open; *funua kitabu*, open a book.
fununu, n. rumour, gossip, hearsay.
funza, ma-, n. jigger,

funzo

maggot. 2. **ku-**, v.t. to teach, to instruct.
funzo, ma-, n. instruction, lesson, teaching.
fupa, n. bone, see **mfupa**.
fupi, adj. short, shallow.
fupisha, ku-, v.t. shorten, abbreviate.
fupisho, ma-, n. abbreviation.
fura, ku-, v.i. swell up, become very upset.
furaha n. joy, *ona furaha*, feel happy; *kwa furaha*, with pleasure.
furahi, ku-, v.i. feel happy, also **furahia**, *tunafurahia siku hii*, we feel happy about this day.
furahia, ku-, v.t. rejoice, be cheerful, bask.
furahifu, adj. happy.
furahisha, ku-, v.t. be delightful, be enjoyable.
furika, ku-, v.i. overflow, *mto umefurika*, the river has overflowed.
fursa, n. opportunity, occasion, chance, *asante kwa fursa hii*, thank you for this opportunity.
furukuta, ku-, v.i. move about, agitate, struggle

fuvu

to free oneself from a certain situation.
furusha, ku-, v.t. drive away, rout.
furushi, ma-, n. parcel.
fuska, ma-, n. adulterer, fornicator.
fususi, n. gem, precious stone.
futa, ku-, v.t. wipe, cancel, wipe off, erase, invalidate, clean up, eradicate, annul 2. draw (pull a knife/sword), unsheath.
futari, n. food normally eaten to bread the fast, foodstuff such as cassava, yams, bananas used during the holy month of Ramadan.
futi, n. knee 2. foot, measuring tape.
futika, ku-, v.i. disappear, be unreadable.
futikamba, n. tape measure.
futuka, ku-, v.i. burge out, stick out.
futuru, ku-, v.i. break a fast mostly during the holy month of Ramadan.
fuvu, ma-, n. skull, shell,

fuvu la kale zaidi la mwanadamu lilivumbuliwa huko Olduvai Gorge, the oldest human skull was discovered at Olduvai Gorge.

fuzu, ku-, v.t. win, succeed, *fuzu mafunzo ya uaskari*, suceed in military training.

fyata, ku-, v.t. feel scared, *mbwa amefyata mkia*, the dog has its tail between its legs, a sign of fright.

fyatua, ku-, v.t. snapshot, make bricks, fire a gun.

fyatuka, ku-, v.i. go off suddenly.

fyeka, ku-, v.t. clear bush, *fyeka msitu*, clear the bush.

fyeko, ma-, n. cleaning, clearing in a bush.

fyonya, ku-, v.t. suck, draw into the mouth, to make a thin sound as a sign of dissatisfaction and anger.

fyonza, ku-, v.t. to suck.

fyosi, adj. insulting.

fyoza, ku-, v.t. insult, joke, kid.

fyuzi, n. fuse.

G

gaagaa, ku-, v.i. toss about, roll over and over.

gadi, n. period on guard, support pole.

gagulo, ma-, n. underdskirt.

gaidi, ma-, n. robber, terrorist, *magaidi wa kimataifa,* international terrorists.

galoni, n. gallon.

gamba, ku-, v.i. *jigamba,* boast, brag.

gamba, ma-, n. scale of fish, shell, bark.

gambusi, ma-, n. mandolin.

ganda, ma-, n. husk, shell; ganda, **ku-,** v.i. coagulate (milk, blood), *maziwa ya kuganda (mgando),* curdled milk, yoghurt.

gandamana, ku-, v.i. stick together.

gandamiza, ku-, v.t. press hard on, oppress.

gandisha, ku-, v.t. clog, affix, bind, coagulate.

gandua, ku-, v.t. pull off.

ganduka, ku-, v.i. peel off, come off.

ganga, ku-, v.t. bind up, treat medically; *ganga jeraha,* bandage a wound.

gangamala, ku-, v.i. persist, insist.

gangua, ku-, v.t. cure, exorcise, remove a magic spell.

gani, interr. pron. what sort, *kitu gani?* what sort of thing? *jinsi gani?* how? *wakati gani?* when? *pahali gani?* where? *habari gani?* what's the news? how are you?

ganja, n. rolled up marijuana.

ganzi, n. numbness, *mguu umekufa ganzi,* the leg is numbed, *tia meno ganzi,* set the teeth on edge, anaesthetisia.

gari, ma-, n. car, *gari la mizigo,* truck, lorry.

gati   ghafi

gati, n. dock, landing place.
gauni, ma-, n. gown, long dress for women.
gavana, ma-, n. governor, *kidhibiti mwendo*, speed governor.
gawa, gawanya, ku-, v.t. appportion, divide; *gawa karata*, deal cards; *gawa nusu kwa nusu*, divide equally, dispense.
gawia, ku-, v.t. distribute to, assign, allocate.
gawio, ma-, n. dividend, talent.
gawo, gawio, ma-, n. portion, rationing, *mgao wa umeme*, power rationing.
gazeti, ma-, n. newspaper.
gegedu, n. cartilage, disc.
gego, ma-, n. molar.
geji, n. gauge.
gema, ku-, v.t. tap the bark of a tree to get its sap or resin, *gema mpira*, tap rubber, gema tembo, tap
genge, ma-, n. gang of workers, the place where they sell vegetables etc, clique, food kiosk, vendor stoll.

geni, adj. strange, *kitu kigeni*, something new, unusual, see **mgeni, wageni**, guest(s).
gereji, ma-, n. garage.
geresha, ku-, v.i. cheat.
gereza, ma-, n. prison.
gesi, n. gas.
geugeu, adj. fickle, unreliable.
geuka, ku-, v.i. change, turn about.
geukia, ku-, v.i. turn and face another direction.
geuza, ku-, v.t. turn over something, *geuza shati lako*, turn your shirt over.
geuzi, ma-, n. change.
geza, ku-, v.t. imitate, attempt.
ghadhabika, (gazabika), ku-, v. be angry, upset.
ghadhabisha, ku-, v.t. make angry, anger somebody.
ghadhabu, n. anger.
ghadhibika, ku-, v.i. be enranged, be furious, be on the rampage.
ghadhibisha, ku-, v.t. exasperate.
ghafi, n. gross weight,

ghafilika   **glukosi**

raw, unprocessed.
ghafilika, ku-, v.i. be forgetful, *ameghafilika tu, si makusudi*; it was an oversight, it was not his intention.
ghafla, n. suddenness, suddenly.
ghaibu, adv. out of sight.
ghairi, ku-, v.i. change one's mind.
ghala, n. storehouse, warehouse, barn.
ghali, adj. expensive, *ni aghali sana*, it is so expensive.
ghani, ku-, v.t. sing, recite.
gharama, n. expenses.
gharika, n. cataclysm, downpour, flood.
gharimia, ku-, v.t. spend on, pay for.
gharimu, ku-, v.t. cost, *imekugharimu shillingi ngapi?* how much did it cost you?
ghashi, n. deception, cheating, lie.
ghasi, ku-, v.t. trouble, bother.
ghasia, n. confusion, disorder, *fanya ghasia*, cause chaos, disorder.
ghaya, n. ecstacy.
ghiliba, n. duplicity.
ghilibu, ku-, v.t. deceive, swindle 2, n. hoodwink, trickery, cunning.
ghorofa, n. story house.
ghuba, n. gulf, Persian gulf, *Ghuba ya Uajemi*.
ghushi, ku-, v.t. cheat, forge.
ghusubu, ku-, v.t. compel.
gia, n. gear, *weka, tia gia*, change gear.
gidamu, n. lace of a sandal, shoe lace.
gilasi, n. glass.
giligili, n. fluid.
gimbi, ma-, n. model, shape.
gingi, vi-, n. peg, stake.
gini, n. guinea.
gitaa, ma-, n. guitar, *piga gitaa*, play the guitar.
giza, n. darkness, *moyo wa mwenzio ni msitu wa giza*; another person's heart is a dark forest, a mystery.
glakoma, n. glaucoma.
glasi, n. glass (drinking).
glovu, n. glove.
glukosi, n. glucose.

gluu, n. glue.
gobori, n. home made gun.
godoro, ma-, n. mattress, *magodoro safi*, good mattresses.
gofu, ma-, n. ruins, golf (game).
gogo, ma-, n. log, *usafirishaji wa magoo*, transportation of logs.
goigoi, n. lazy person, *usiwe goigoi*, don't be lazy.
goli, ma-, n. goal (sport), *funga goli*, score a goal.
golikipa, ma-, n. goal-keeper.
gololi, n. ball of glass for playing.
goma, ku-, v.i. go on strike, refuse to comply; *walimu wamegoma*, teachers are on strike, resist, obect to something.
gomba, ku-, v.i. scold, call to task.
gombana, ku-, v.t. be in bad terms with one another, fight one another.
gombea, ku-, v.t. quarrel over something 2. campaign for a political post, *anagombea ubunge*, he is contesting a parliamentary seat.
gombeza, ku-, v.t. reprimand, scold, *anagombeza watoto*, he(she) is scolding children.
gomboa, ku-, v.t. redeem people or property from sb.
gome, ma-, n. bark of trees.
gomvi, adj. quarrelsome.
gonga, ku-, v.t. knock at, *gonga mlango*, knock at a door, to hit something.
gongana, ku-, v.t. to collide with one another, *magari yamegongana*, cars have collided with one another.
gongo, ma-, n. club, big stick 2. illicit alcoholic drink.
gonjwa, m-, wa-, n. a patient, sick, *mtu mgonjwa*, a sick person.
gorofa, n. see **orofa**.
gota, ku-, v.t. rap, knock 2. stick, refuse to move.

goti   gwiji

goti, ma-, knee, *piga magoti*, kneel, *pigia magoti mfalme*, kneel in front of the king.

govi, n. foreskin of a penis when uncircumcised.

gramafoni, n. gramaphone (musical instrument).

gramu, n. gramme (smallest weighing scale).

grisi, n. grease.

guberi, n. prostitute, *guberi mfawidhi*, professional prostitute.

gubika, ku-, v.t. cover from head to toe, cover completely.

gubu, n. annoyance, unnecessary disturbance, *gubu la mke*, annoyance by a wife.

gudulia, ma-, n. water jar.

gugu, ma-, n. weed, thicket.

gugumiza, ku-, v.i. stammer

gugumizi, ma-, n. one who stammers.

guguna, ku-, v.t. gnaw, nibble.

gulio, ma-, n. special open market opened on specific days only.

gumba, adj. sterile, *kidole gumba*, thumb, barren.

gumu, adj. difficult, hard, *kazi ngumu*, hard work.

gumzo, n. chat, talk-about.

guna, ku-, v.i. grumble.

gundi, n. glue, *gundi ya maji*, fluid glue.

gundua, ku-, v.t. discover, *gundua siri*, unveil a secret.

gunzi, ma-, n. corn cob.

guru, adj. *sukari guru*, unrefined sugar.

gurudumu, ma-, n. wheel.

gusa, ku-, v.t. touch, *hadithi inayogusa*, a very touching (moving) story.

gusia, ku-, v.t. mention sth, use sth to touch another person or thing.

guta, ma-, n. three wheeled cycles used for carrying loads.

gutua, ku-, v.t. startle.

gutuka, ku-, v.i. be startled, wake up about.

gutusha, ku-, v.t. startle.

gwadu, adj. sour taste.

gwaride, n. parade, drill.

gwiji, adj. somebody who is good at sth, master in a certain area (field).

H

ha! interj. expression of surprise or dismay, *ha! Amekosa goli,* oh! He has missed a goal.

haba, adj. few (prov.), *haba na haba hujaza kibaba,* small strokes fell great oaks, little by little fills

habari, n. news, *habari gani?* how are you?

hadaa, ku-, v.t. hoodwink, cheat 2. n. trickery.

hadaika, ku-, v.i. be cheated.

hadhara, n. the public, audience, *hadharani,* in public.

hadhari, adv. care, precaution.

hadhi, n. dignity, honour, status, *mvunjie mtu hadhi,* disgrace somebody.

hadi, prep. until, to, *hadi sasa hajaonekana,* until now he has not appeared.

hadithi, n. story, tale, *hadithi ya kutunga,* fiction.

hadithia, ku-, v. narrate a story, *bibi huhadithia hadithi tamu,* grandmother narrates good stories.

hafifu, adj. of poor quality, faint.

hafla, n. celebration, party.

haha, ku-, v.i. to palpitate, to scrumble about, wonder anxiously.

haiba, n. personality, *haiba nzuri,* good personality, attractive charm.

haidhuru, v.i. neg. it does not matter, no problem, nevertheless.

haini, wa-, n. conspirator, betrayer, *angamiza wahaini,* get rid of conspirators.

haja, n. need, *enda haja,* attend to nature's call, *haina haja,* there is no need for it.

hajambo, v.i. form, he, she is well.
hajiri, ku-, v.i. emigrate.
haki, n. right, *haki za binadamu*, human rights, *tetea haki yako*, fight for your right, *haki ya kupiga kura*, franchise.
hakika, adj. certain, to be sure, *ni hakika atakuja*, he is certainly coming.
hakiki, ku-, v.t. make a critical review.
hakikisha, ku-, v.t. make sure, ascertain, confirm.
hakikishia, ku-, v.t. guarantee.
hakikisho, n. critique, confirmation.
hakimu, ma-, n. judge, magistrate.
halafu, adv. afterwards, then, later, *halafu akasema*, then he said.
halaiki, n. multitude, mass, crowd, *mauaji ya halaiki*, genocide, mass killings.
halali, adj. lawful (opp. **haramu**) 2. he, she does not sleep.
halalisha, ku-, v.t. render lawful, allow, officiate.

haleluya, interj. alleluia, hallelujah, praise the Lord, see also **aleluya**.
hali, n. condition, *hali ya hewa*, the weather condition, *hali yake si nzuri*, he, she is not
halifu, ku-, v.t. commit crime, *mhalifu*, criminal.
halisi, adj. genuine, original, pure, authentic, *spea halisi*, genuine parts.
halmashauri, n. council.
halua, n. sweetmeat for chewing.
hama, ku-, v.i. emigrate, move from one place to another.
hamaki, ku-, v.i. act on the spur of the moment, *usihamaki*, don't rush, take time.
hamaki, ku-, v.i. be intrigued, be enraged.
hamali, ma-, n. coolie.
hamanisha, ku-, v.i. discompose.
hamasa, n. strong desire to make more effort in doing something.
hamasisha, ku-, v.t. mobilise, intistigate.

hamia, ku-, v.i. move to a new place or house, *wamehamia Moshi,* they have moved to Moshi.

hamira, n. leaven, yeast, baking powder.

hamu, n. desire, longing for something, *nina hamu ya kuwaona wazazi wangu,* I long to see my parents.

handaki, ma-, n. ditch, dike, trench, *chimba handaki,* dig a ditch.

hangaika, ku-, v.i. worry about, feel uneasy.

hani, ku-, v.i. condole.

hanithi, ma-, n. impotent, a persnon not able to perform the sexual act, functionless.

hapa, adv. here, *hapahapa,* at this very place, *hapa na pale,* here and there.

hapana, adv. of negation, there is not, no.

hara, ku-, v.i. have loose bowels, see **harisha.**

haradali, n. mustard, *mbegu ya haradali,* mustard seed.

haraka, n. haste, *fanya haraka,* hurry up, *harakaharaka haina baraka,* (lit.) hurry, hurry has no blessing, more haste less speed (prov).

harakisha, ku-, v.i. hasten, make hurry.

haramia, ma-, n. pirate, robber.

haramisha, ku-, v.t. make illegal, prohibit.

haramu, adj. illegal, prohibited, *haya ni maandamano haramu,* this is an illegal procession.

haribifu, adj. destructive.

haribika, ku-, v.i. go bad, rot.

haribu, ku-, v.t. destroy, corrupt.

hariri, ku-, v.t. edit, *hariri muswada,* edit a manuscript.

harufu, n. smell, *harufu mbaya,* bad smell.

harusi, n. wedding celebration/ ceremony.

hasa, adv. especially.

hasara, n. loss, *pata hasara,* incur a loss.

hasha, interj. *la hasha,* not

hasi   heshima

at all.
hasi, ku-, v.t. castrate 2. negative.
hasimu, ma-, n. enemy, opponent.
hasira, n. anger, *hasira hasara*, anger is a bad adviser, *hasira kali*, fury.
hata, prep. not, *hata kidogo*, not at all, *hata ufanye nini sikubali*, no matter what you do I won't accept.
hatamu, n. bridle, *shika hatamu*, take control, hold the reins.
hatari, n. danger.
hatarisha, ku-, v.i. endanger.
hati, n. writing, hand writing, document.
hatia, n. crime, *ana hatia*, he is guilty.
hatihati, n. kind of tension.
hatimaye, adv. afterwards, in the end.
hatimkato, n. secretarial art, shorthand.
hatua, n. step, *ni hatua kutoka hapa*, it is a distance from here.
hawa, dem. pron. these people 2. n. *Hawa*, Eve, first woman, wife of Adam.
haya, n. shame, *ona haya*, feel shy.
hazina, n. treasure.
hebu, n. well then, *hebu njoo*, please come here.
hedhi, n. menstruation.
hekaheka, n. chaos, hectic movement.
hekalu, n. temple.
hekima, n. wisdom, prudence.
hema, ku-, v.i. breathe in and out 2. n. tent, *piga hema*, pitch a tent.
hereni, n. earings, *hereni za dhahabu*, golden earings.
heri, n. bliss, good luck, *heri yako*, you're lucky, *kwa heri*, good bye, *Heri ya Krismasi*, Merry Christmas.
herufi, n. letter a, b, c, etc.
hesabu, n. arithmetic, sum 2. v.t. count.
heshima, n. honour, respect, *ona heshima*, feel honoured; *toa heshima za mwisho*, pay the last respects to

heshimu   hodari

somebody dead.

heshimu, ku-, v.t. pay due respect, honour.

hewa, n. air, *vuta hewa,* breathe in, *punga hewa,* go for a walk.

hewala, interj. okay, alright, *hewala bwana,* okay sir.

hiari, n. choice, *hiari yako,* its your choice, as you like, consent.

hifadhi, ku-, v.t. preserve 2. n. reserve.

hija, n. pilgrimage, *nchi ya hija,* pilgrimage land.

hijabu, n. clothes worn by Moslem women that resemble baibui.

hila, n. trick, *kwa hila,* cunningly, duplicity, fraud.

himaya, n. monopoly, trusteeship.

himiza, ku-, v.t. hurry on somebody, to urge on, facilitate.

hindi, ma-, n. maize.

hirizi, n. talisman, amulet, *vaa hirizi kujikinga,* put on amulets to protect oneself.

hisa, n. share in a business.

hisani, n. kindness, *kwa hisani yako,* with your kindness.

hisi, ku-, v.t. feel, perceive.

historia, n. history, *historia ya Wamasai,* the Maasai history.

hitaji, ku-, v.t. want, feel a need for something 2. n. **ma-,** needs.

hitajiana, ku-, v.t. need one another.

hitilafiana, ku-, v.i. differ, *tumehitilafiana katika jambo hili,* we have differed on this point.

hitilafu, n. difference, flaw.

hitimisha, ku-, v.t. end, conclude.

hitimu, ku-, v. graduate, come to the end of ones studies.

hivi, adv. in this way, *fanya hivi,* do it in this way, *sasa hivi,* just now, right now.

hivyo, adv. in this manner, *fanya hivyohivyo,* do it exactly, in like manner.

hodari, adj. brave, *mwalimu hodari,* a very

hodi   husisha

capable teacher, be good at something.

hodi, interj. greeting before entering a house, is anyone in?

hofu, n. great fear, apprehension 2. **ku-**, v.i. fear.

hohehahe, adj. very poor, in destitute condition.

hoi, adj. very ill, *yu hoi*, he is very ill.

hoja, n. argument, point, *hiyo si hoja*, that is not an issue.

hoji, ku-, v.t. interview, cross-examine, interrogate.

homa, n. fever, *ana homa*, he has fever; *pata homa*, fall sick.

honga, ku-, v.t. give a bribe.

hongera, n. congratulation.

hongo, n. bribe, *pokea hongo*, receive a bribe, *toa hongo*, give a bribe.

hostia, n. host (Roman Catholic).

hotuba, n. speech, *toa hotuba*, give a speech.

huba, n. affection, love, passion.

hubiri, ku-, v.i. preach, *hubiri Neno la Mungu*, preach the word of God, proclaim.

hudhuria, ku-, v.t. attend, *hudhuria masomo*, attend lectures, lessons.

hudhurungi, n. yellowish brown.

huduma, n. service, *pata huduma*, be served.

hudumia, ku-, v.t. serve, *hudumia wateja*, serve customers.

hukumu, ku-, v.t. judge, condemn, *alihukumiwa kifo*, he was condemned to death.

humo, adv. inside there, *baki humo humo*, remain right there.

huni, ku-, v.i. wander about deviantly.

huruma, n. mercy, *ona huruma*, feel pity, *onea huruma*, feel pity for.

husiana, ku-, v.t. relate with, about sth.

husika, ku-, v.i. be concerned, *huhusiki*, you are not involved in it.

husisha, ku-, v.t. relate with, connect with, join with.

husu 　　　　　　　　　　　huzunisha

husu, ku-, v.i. concern, *inahusu nini?* what is it all about?
husuda, n. jealousy, envy, *ona husuda,* feel envy.
hutubia, ku-, v.t. preach to, make sermon to.
hutubu, ku-, v.t. make sermony, preach.
huzuni, n. sorrow, grief.
huzunika, ku-, v.i. be sad, *usihuzunike,* don't be sad.
huzunisha, ku-, v.t. cause grief, sadden, humiliate.

I

iba, ku-, v.t. steal, *mwizi ameiba*, the thief has stolen.
ibada, n. religious ceremony, *ibada ya Misa*, service mass, liturgy.
ibia, ku-, v.t. steal from, *amekuibia nini?* what has he stolen from you?
ibilisi, ma-, n. satan, devil, scapegoat for wrong doings, *ni ilibilisi alinishika*, it's the devil that occupied me.
ibua, ku-, v.t. bring up from underneath/below, cause to emerge.
ibuka, ku-, v.i. crop up, come up, emerge.
idadi, n. quantity, amount.
idara, n. department, *unafanya kazi idara gani?* in which department do you work?
idhaa, n. radio programme, *idhaa ya Kiswahili*, Kiswahili programme.
idhini, n. permit, consent, *tunahitaji idhini ya mgonjwa*, we need the consent of the sick.
idhinisha, ku-, v.t. permit, authorise, *idhinisha malipo*, authorise payment.
iga, ku-, v.t. imitate, mirror.
igiza, ku-, v.t. act in a theatre, imitate.
ijapokuwa, conj. even though, although.
Ijumaa, n. Friday.
ikiwa, prep. if, in case.
ikulu, n. State House, White House.
ikweta, n. equator, *Kusini mwa Ikweta*, South of Equator.
ila, n. defect 2. prep. except.
ilani, n. notice, manifesto, *ilani ya uchaguzi*, elections manifesto.
ili, prep. so that, in order to, *ili ufanikiwe fanya bidii*, in order to succeed

ilimradi

you must make an effort.

ilimradi, conj. so long as, *ilimradi uwe hapa mapema*, so long as you come back here early.

imamu, ma-, n. a moslem leader who leads the prayers.

imani, n. faith, belief, *hiyo ni imani yako*, that is your belief.

imara, adj. firm, strong, stable, unshakable.

imarisha, ku-, v.t. strengthen, enforce.

imba, ku-, v.i. sing, ham (sing with closed mouth, buzz like a bee).

imbisha, ku-, v.t. lead a singing group, choir, conduct a choir or a singing group.

imla, n. dictation, *zoezi la imla*, dictation exercise.

inama, ku-, v.i. bend, turn face down.

inamia, ku-, v. lean on, bend on.

inamisha, cause to bend, *inamisha kichwa*, bow down.

inchi, n. inch, *inchi tano*, five inches.

inukia

ingawa, ingawaje, conj. although, eventhough.

ingia, ku-, v.i. enter, *ingia ndani*, get in.

ingilia, ku-, v.t. intervene, *ingilia kati*, intervene, interfere, interrupt.

ingiza, ku-, v.t. put into, take in, cause to enter, *ingiza kidole*, put your finger into it.

ingizo, ma-, n. entry, inclusion.

ini, ma-, n. liver, *kata maini*, hurt the feelings of somebody.

injili, n. gospel, good news.

injini, n. engine.

insha, n. essay, composition, *mashindano ya insha*, essay competition.

inua, ku-, v.t. lift up, put up, elevate, *inua mikono*, raise the hands up.

inuka, ku-, v.i. get up, rise.

inukia, ku-, v.i. come up, grow in business/ professionwise.

iodini, n. iodine.
ipi, adj. which, *kitabu kipi*, which book?
isha, ku-, v.i. be finished, *shauri limekwisha*, the case is over, finished.
ishara, n. sign, token, symbol, *ishara ya nyakati*, signs of time.
ishi, ku-, v.i. live, *unaishi wapi?* where do you live?
ishia, ku-, v.i. end in, *jambo limeishia wapi?* how has the matter ended?
ishirini, n. twenty.
ishiwa, ku-, v.t. be short of sth, be bankrupt.
isimu, n. linguistics, *somea isimu*, study linguistics.
isipokuwa, prep. except, unless.
ita, ku-, v.t. call, *ita mkutano*, call a meeting.
itifaki, n. protocol, *Itifaki ya Kyoto*, the Kyoto Protocol.
itika, itikia, ku-, v.i answer a call, *itikia wito*, respond to a call.
itikadi, n. ideology, philosophy of life.
itikia, see **itika**, respond to a call.
itisha, ku-, v.t. call to a meeting, *itisha mkutano*, call people to a meeting.
itwa, ku-, v.i. be called, named, *unaitwa nani?* what is your name?
iva, ku-, v.i. become ripe, come to a head, *chakula kimeiva*, the food is ready.
ivisha, ku-, v.t. cause to ripen, *ivisha matunda kwa moshi*, cause fruits to be ripe by using smoke.
iwapo, conj. if, in case, *iwapo utamwona mwambie aje*, if you see him tell him to come here.

J

ja, ku-, v.i. come, *anakuja*, he is coming. 2. *hajaja*, he has not arrived.

jaa, ku-, v.i be filled up, *maji yamejaa mtoni*, the river is full of water.

jabali, ma-, n. rock.

jadi, n. tradition, *dawa za jadi*, traditional medicine.

jadili, ku-, v.i. discuss, exchange views.

jagi, ma-, n. jug.

jahanamu, n. hell.

jahazi, ma-, n. dhow, boat.

jaji, ma-, n. judge 2. **ku-,** v.t. judge sb.

jaketi, ma-, n. jacket.

jalada, ma-, n. cover of a book, file, folder.

jalala, ma-, n. dumping place.

jali, ku-, v.t. to care for, to care about, *hajali kitu*, he does not care about anything.

jalia, ku-, v.t. bestow upon, bless with, confer, *alipewa heshima*, honour was conferred upon him.

jaliwa, ku-, v.i. be talented, be gifted, *amejaliwa*, he/she is gifted.

jaluba, ma-, n. bed of rice, *majaluba matano*, five beds of rice.

jamaa, n. family, kin, *jamani!* oh, dear!

jamba, ku-, v.i. fart, give out bad gas through the annul.

jambazi, ma-, n. robber, bandit, gunman.

jambia, ma-, n. sword.

jambo, mambo, n. matter, affair 2. hello!

jamhuri, n. republic, *Siku ya Jamhuri*, Republic Day.

jamii, n. society, community, *Jamii ya Watanzania*, Tanzanian Society.

jamiiana, ku-, v.i. have sex

jamvi   **jeraha**

with somebody, sexual intercourse.

jamvi, n. mat made of reeds.

jana, adv. yesterday, *mwaka jana*, last year.

jando, n. rite of initiation, *yuko jandoni*, he is undergoing the rite of initiation.

janga, ma-, n. calamity, disaster.

jangili, ma-, n. poacher.

jangwa, ma-, n. desert, arid land, *Jangwa la Sahara*, the Sahara Desert.

jani, ma-, n. grass, leaf.

janja, adj. clever, tricky.

Januari, n. January.

japo, prep. although, *kipya kinyemi japo kidonda* (saying), something new is very good although in the end it may be very costful.

jaribio, ma-, n. trial, attempt, test.

jaribu, ku-, v.t. try out something.

jasho, n. sweat, *toa jasho*, perspire.

jasiri, n. brave person 2. adj. brave, bold, courageous, *uwe jasiri*, be courageous.

jasusi, ma-, n. spy.

jaza, ku-, v.t. fill in, *jaza maji*, fill with water.

jazba, n. uncontrolled emotion, emotional reaction (negative).

je, interrog. how? *je, utakuja*? well, are you coming? *unasemaje*? what do you say?

jedwali, ma-, n. table that shows certain datas.

jeki, n. jack.

jela, n. prison, remand.

jembe, ma-, n. hoe, plough.

jemedari, ma-, n. top rank in the army, marshal.

jenerali, ma-, n. rank of general in the army.

jenereta, ma-, n. generator, see also **kanguvuke**.

jeneza, ma-, n. coffin.

jenga, ku-, v.t. build, erect, *jenga nyumba*, build a house, construct.

jengo, ma-, n. building, edifice.

jeraha, ma-, n. wound, ulcer.

jeruhi   jikinga

jeruhi, ku-, v.t. hurt, wound.

jeshi, ma-, n. army, *jeshi la anga*, air force, *jeshi la majini*, navy, corps.

jeuri, adj. arrogant, *fanya jeuri*, act arrogantly, *hana jeuri hiyo*, he dare not do that.

jiachia, ku-, v.i. let oneself free.

jialika, ku-, v.t. have oneself invited.

jiamini, ku-, v.t. be confident with oneself.

jiamulia, ku-, v.i. decide freely on sth by oneself.

jiandikisha, ku-, v.t. enrol oneself, have oneself registered.

jibanza, ku-, v.t. press oneself very close to a wall or tree or anything.

jibini, n. cheese.

jibu, ma-, n. answer 2. **ku-,** v.t. give an answer.

jicho, macho, n. eye, eyes, *kaa macho*, be alert, *tupia jicho*, keep an eye on.

jidai, ku-, v.i. boast, *anajidai nini?* what is he boasting about?

jidhalilisha, ku-, v.i. condescend.

jiendeleza, ku-, v.t. make oneself better in certain areas, develop ones talents.

jifungua, ku-, v.t. deliever, give birth.

jifunza, ku-, v.i. study, learn.

jigamba, ku-, v.i. brag, boast.

jigeuza, ku-, v.t. turn oneself around, disguise oneself.

jigonga, ku-, v.t. have oneself hit by sth.

jihadhari, ku-, v.i. take care.

jihadi, n. jihad, war to spread Islamic faith.

jihusisha, ku-, v.t. have oneself take part in sth, putting ones nose into sth.

jiji, n. city, *Jiji la Dar es Salaam*, the City of Dar es Salaam.

jike, ma-, n. female animal.

jikinga, ku-, v.t. protect oneself, defend oneself from harm.

jiko, ma-, n. kitchen, stove, cooker, *jiko la umeme*, electric cooker 2. n. wife, *amepata jiko*, he has got married.
jiko, meko, n. kitchen.
jikosha, ku-, v.i. justify one's conduct.
jimbo, ma-, n. province, region.
jina, ma-, n. name.
jinai, adj. criminal, *kosa la jinai*, criminal offence.
jinga, adj. foolish.
jini, ma-, n. jinn, *ana jini*, she is possessed (with a jinn).
jino, meno, n. tooth, teeth.
jinsi, n. sort, *jinsi gani?* what sort? how?
jinsia, n. gender, sex.
jinyima, ku-, v.t. self denial, abstain oneself from.
jiografia, n. geography.
jiona, ku-, v.i. boast.
jioni, n. evening, in the evening, *mlo wa jioni*, evening meal.
jipongeza, ku-, v.t. congratulate oneself.
jipu, ma-, n. boil, absess.
jirani, ma-, n. neighbour.
jisaidia, ku-, v.t. relieve oneself, attend to nature's call.
jishusha, ku-, v.i. condescend.
jitahidi, ku-, v.i. make efforts, exert oneself, *jitihada*, n. effort.
jitenga, ku-, v.t. seclude oneself, separate from the main body, break from the main body.
jitoa, ku-, v.t. withdraw from, refuse to go on.
jitu, ma-, n. giant.
jitwalia, ku-, v.t. usurp, take forcefully, grab.
jiuzulu, ku-, v.t. retire, resign from, *amejiuzulu*, he has resigned from.
jivu, ma-, n. ashes.
jivuna, ku-, v.i. boast, be proud of oneself.
jiwe, mawe, n. stone, *piga mtu mawe*, stone someone.
jizatiti, ku-, v.t. prepare oneself/group well for a certain occassion/event.
jogoo, ma-, n. cock, *jogoo limewika*, the cock has crowed.

jongea — juzuu

jongea, ku-, v.i. come nearer, come forward, approach towards something or somebody.

jongoo, n. milliped.

jora, ma-, n. roll of cloth.

joto, n. heat, *sikia joto,* feel hot.

jozi, ma-, n. pair, *jozi ya viatu,* a pair of shoes.

jua, n. the sun 2. **ku-,** v.t. know, *unajuaje?* how do you know? *je, unajua Kiswahili?* do you speak Kiswahili?

judo, n. judo.

juha, ma-, n. simpleton.

juju, n. juju, withcraft power.

jukumu, ma-, n. obligation, responsibility.

jukwaa, ma-, n. platform.

Julai, n. July.

julikana, ku-, v.i. be known, *anajulikana vizuri,* he is well known.

julisha, ku-, v.t. inform, introduce.

juma, ma-, n. week, *Jumamosi,* Saturday, *Jumapili,* Sunday, *Jumatatu,* Monday, *Jumanne,* Tuesday, *Jumatano,* Wednesday, *Alhamisi,* Thursday, *Ijumaa,* Friday.

jumbe, wa-, n. headman, delegates, members.

jumla, n. total, sum.

jumlisha, ku-, v.t. add.

jumuia, n. community, association, *Jumuia Ndogondogo za Kikristu,* Small Christian Communities.

jumuika, ku-, v.t. sociate with the others.

Juni, n. June.

juta, ku-, v.i. regret, be sorry for one's mistakes.

juto, ma-, n. remorse.

juu, adv. aloft.

juujuu, adj. & adv. superficial, superficially.

juzi, n. day before yesterday, *nilionana naye juzi,* I met him/her day before yesterday.

juzijuzi, majuzi, n. a few days ago, a short period ago.

juzuu, ma-, n. chapter of Quran.

K

ka, used to show past tense after li has been used, *aliondoka akaenda mjini*, he left and went to town.

kaa, ku-, v.i. stay, sit down, settle down, *unakaa wapi?* where do you stay? *anakaa mjini*, he lives in town.

kaa, m-, n. coal, *kaa la moto*, glowing embers.

kaakaa, ku-, v.i. wait a while, be stranded.

kaanga, ku-, v.t. fry, *kaanga nyama*, roast meat; *mayai ya kukaanga*, fried eggs.

kaba, ku-, v.t. choke, *kaba koo*, throttle.

kababu, n. kebab, meat ball.

kabaila, ma-, n. landlord, feudalist, feudal lord.

kabati, ma-, n. cupboard.

kabichi, n. cabbage.

kabidhi, ku-, v.i. hand over, *kabidhi madaraka*, hand over power.

kabila, ma-, n. tribe, genus, people/things of the same origin.

kabili, ku-, v.t. confront, face somebody; *kabiliana na adui*, confront the enemy.

kabisa, adv. completely, absolutely, *lazima niende kabisa*, no choice, I have to go.

kabla, conj. before, *kabla ya*, before something.

kabrasha, ma-, n. documents needed for a meeting/workshop/seminar.

kabureta, n. carburetor.

kaburi, ma-, n. grave, cemetery.

kaburu, ma-, n. boers of South Africa.

kabwela, ma-, n. people with little or no income.

kachero, ma-, n. spy, detective.

kachumbari, n. tomato mixed with onions and cabbage, raddish, a salad

kada

of finely chopped tomato, onion, cabbage, garlic and pepper used with roast meat, relish.

kada, n. cadre.

kadha wa kadha, adv. etc. and so on.

kadhaa, adj. a few, *watu kadhaa walifika*, a few people came.

kadhalika, adv. likewise, *na kadhalika*, etc.

kadhia, n. misfortunes haunting a person.

kadi, n. card, *kadi nyekundu*, a red card.

kadinali, n. cardinal.

kadiri, n. amount, *kadiri gani?* how much? approximate size, amount.

kadiria, ku-, v.t. estamate sth.

kadiria, ku-, v.t. estimate, reckon.

kadirio, ma-, n. estimation, estimate.

kafara, n. sacrifice, victim.

kafeteria, n. cafeteria.

kafiri, ma-, n. non-believer in God, atheist, infidel.

kagua, ku-, v.t. inspect, *kagua shule*, inspect a school.

kahaba, ma-, n. prostitute, harlot.

kahawa, n. coffee, *je, utakunywa kahawa?* will you have some coffee?

kaidi, ku-, v.i. be obstinate 2. adj. disobedient, *mtoto huyu ni mkaidi*, this child is disobedient, head strong.

kaimu, n, deputy, acting, vice, 2. **ku-**, v. to deputise.

kaka, n. elder brother, *huyu ni kaka yangu wa kufikia*, this is my step brother.

kakakuona, n. pangolin, a creature that is used to foretell future events.

kakamavu, adj. alert and strong, smart, *eneo la ukakamavu*, smart area.

kakao, n. cocoa.

kakasi, adj. aciduous, taste of unripe mango.

kalamu, n. pen, *kalamu ya mkaa*, pencil.

kale, n. antiquity, *mambo ya kale*, past events, antiques; *hapo kale*, once upon a time, *zamani za kale*, in ancient times.

kalenda, n. calendar.

kali, adj. sharp, *kisu si kikali*, the knife is not sharp 2. adj. strict, *baba yake ni mkali sana*, his father is very strict.

kalia, ku-, v.t. sit on.

kalisha, ku-, v.t. cause to sit down.

kalisi, n. chalice.

Kalivari, n. Calvary.

kalvati, ma-, n. calvert.

kama, conj. if 2. as, like; *analia kama mtoto*, he cries like a child; *kama nini?* like what? 3. v. press out, *kama ng'ombe*, milk a cow, see also **kamua**.

kamambe, adj. super, of a high quality, enormous.

kamanda, ma-, n. commander.

kamandoo, ma-, n. commando.

kamari, n. gambling, *mcheza kamari*, a gambler.

kamasi, ma-, n. mucus from the nose when one has flue.

kamata, ku-, v.t. catch, hold, also **shika**, ku-, *kamata mwizi*, catch a thief.

kamati, n. committee, *kamati ya mapatano*, reconciliation committee.

kamba, n. rope, *funga kamba*, tie with a rope.

kambare, n. catfish.

kambi, n. camp, *piga kambi*, pitch camp; *vunja kambi*, break camp.

kambo, n. *mama wa kambo*, step mother, *baba wa kambo*, step father.

kame, adj. dry, arid, desolate, waste.

kamera, n. camera.

kamili, adj. complete, perfect, *hakuna mtu aliye kamili*, nobody is perfect.

kamilifu, adj. see **kamili**.

kamilika, ku-, v.i. be perfect, complete.

kamilisha, ku-, v.t. consummate, complete something, *kamilisha ujenzi*, complete the construction.

kamisaa   kanusha

kamisaa, n. commissar.
kampeni, n. campaign, *kampeni za uchaguzi*, election campaigns.
kampuni, ma-, n. company, firm.
kamua, ku-, v.t. milk, squeeze out.
kamusi, n. dictionary.
kamwe, adv. by no means, never, *sitakusahau kamwe*, I will never forget you.
kana, ku-, v.t. deny, denounce 2.conj. as if.
kanali, ma-, n. colonel.
kanchiri, n. brassiere, *kanchiri nyeupe*, a white brassiere.
kanda, ku-, v.t. press, *kanda unga*, knead dough (fig.), massage.
kanda, n. tape, cassette 2. n. zone, *kanda ya Mashariki*, eastern zone.
kandambili, n. slipper, flip-flop.
kandamiza, ku-, v.t. oppress, apply pressure on.
kandanda, n. football game, soccer, *mashabiki wa kandanda*, football fans.
kandarasi, n. contractor.
kande, ma-, n. cooked maize, mixed with beans.
kandika, ku-, v.t. plaster.
kandili, n. lantern.
kando, n. side, *kando ya mto*; bank of a river, *simama kando*, stand aside, *kandokando ya mto*, along the river.
kanga, n. cotton cloth printed colourful usually with a witty message printed on it worn by women in Tanzania/Kenya 2. guinea fowl.
kanganya, ku-, v.i. confuse, *jambo hili linakanganya*, this matter is confusing.
kangara, n. alcohol made of honey, maize etc.
kanguvuke, n. generator.
kaniki, n. light black cotton cloth.
kanisa, ma-, n. church.
kantini, n. canteen.
kanuni, n. rule, formula, guide line, criterion.
kanusha, ku-, v.t. deny,

kanya

amekanusha mashtaka, he has denied the charges, contradict, confute.

kanya, ku-, v.t. rebuke, give a strong warning, forbid.

kanyaga, ku-, v.t. step on, trample down.

kanyagio, ma-, n. pedal.

kanzu, ma-, n. kaftan, cassock.

kapa, adv. win nothing, lose; *enda kapa,* lose badly in a card game (fig.), gain nothing.

kapera, ma-, n. unmarried man, a bachelor.

kapi, ma-, n. husks, chaff.

kapteni, ma-, n. captain, pilot.

kaptura, n. shorts.

kapu, ma-, n. big basket sewn of reeds.

kaputi, n. to be near death, *nusu kaputi,* anaesthetic.

karafuu, n. clove(s), *mashamba ya karafuu,* clove plantations.

karagosi, vi-, n. puppet, caricuture, cartoon, *mchora vikaragosi,* cartoonist.

karibu

karaha, n. aversion, distaste.

karai, ma-, n. washbasin.

karakana, n. workshop.

karama, n. honour, esteem, talent.

karamu, n. feast, banquet, *fanya karamu,* give a party.

karanga, n. peanuts, *siagi ya karanga,* peanut butter, groundnuts.

karani, ma-, n. clerk, secretary.

karata, n. playing cards, *gawa karata,* deal cards, *cheza karata,* play cards.

karatasi, n. paper.

karibia, ku-, v.i come closer, approach a certain place/thing.

karibiana, ku-, v.t. be close to one another, be almost similar, be almost of the same height.

karibisha, ku-, v.t. welcome, receive guests, *karibisha chakula,* offer food, welcome to a meal.

karibisho, ma-, n. welcome.

karibu, adv. near, *ni*

karimu   katakata

karibu sana, it is very near, *karibu yangu*, *karibu nami*, nearby me, near me. 2. interj. come in, (answer to hodi) (plural), *karibuni*.

karimu, adj. generous, *ni watu wakarimu*, they are generous people.

karipia, ku-, v.t. reproach, admonish.

karipio, ma-, n. rebuke, reprimand.

kariri, ku-, v.t. repeat, recite.

karne, n. century.

karo, n. fee, *ada ya mitihani*, examination fee.

karoti, n. carrot.

kasa, n. sea-turtle.

kasaro, adv. less, *saa sita kasarobo*, a quarter to twelve.

kaseti, n. cassette.

kasha, ma-, n. box, case.

kashata, n. nougat, sugar mixed with coconut flesh and cooked together, sometimes groundnuts cooked with sugar.

kashifu, ku-, v.t. slander, offend, disparage.

kasi, n. haste, *kwa kasi sana*, very fast.

kasino, n. casino.

kasirika, ku-, v.i. get angry, enrage.

kasirisha, ku-, v.t. annoy, infuriate.

kasisi, ma-, n. priest.

kaskazini, n. north.

kasoro, n. defect, *kuna kasoro hapa*, something is wrong here.

kasri, n. palace.

kasuku, n. parrot.

kasumba, n. a complex of any sort, wrong idea about something, mentality, *hiyo ni kasumba mbaya*, that is a bad mentality.

kaswende, n. syphillis.

kata, ku-, v.t. cut, *kata miti*, fell trees; *kata kuni*, chop firewood; *kata shauri*, decide a case; *kata tamaa*, lose hope, despair.

kataa, ku-, v.t. refuse, reject, deny, *kataa katakata*, refuse completely.

katakata, ku-, v.t. cut to pieces.

75

katakombe   kauli

katakombe, ma-, n. catacomb.

katalia, ku-, v.t. refuse something to somebody 2. refuse to move, *amemkatalia ruhusa*, he refused her permission, *mwanamke amekataa kuondoka nyumbani kwa wazazi wake*, she has refused to depart from her parents home.

katalogi, n. catalogue.

katani, n. sisal.

kataza, ku-, v.t. forbid, embargo.

katazo, ma-, n. prohibition.

katekisimu, n. catechism, catholic teachings.

katekista, ma-, n. catechist, catholic teacher teaching the catechism.

kati, katikati, n. middle, centre, *katikati ya barabara*, right in the middle of the road; *weka mpira kati* or *katikati*, put the ball in the centre.

katiba, n. constitution, *masuala ya katiba*, constitutional matters.

katibu, ma-, n. secretary, *katibu muhtasi*, personal secretary.

katika, prep. in, at, *katika kitabu hiki*, in this book. 2. **ku-,** v.i stop functioning, *maji yamekatika*, water is not flowing in the pipes.

katikati, see **kati**.

katili, adj. cruel, brute.

katiza, ku-, v.t. interrupt, *katiza maneno*, break in on a conversation, go across, *katiza barabara*, go across the road.

kato, ma-, n. reduction, fragment.

katoliki, adj. catholic, *kanisa katoliki*, the catholic church.

katoni, n. carton, *katoni tatu*, three cartons..

katua, ku-, v.t. dig in the garden or farm.

katuni, vi-, n. cartoon.

kauka, ku-, v.i. dry up, *sauti imemkauka*, he has lost his voice.

kauli, n. opinion, view, *kauli yake ni hii*, this is his view, a given word,

kaunta   kengele

kauli ya mwisho, last word.
kaunta, n. counter.
kauri, n. cowrie.
kausha, ku-, v.t. cause to dry up, expose to the sun.
kauzu, n. sardines.
kavu, adj. dry, *mti mkavu*, dry wood.
kawaida, n. ordinary, normal, *mambo ya kawaida*, ordinary matters, *kwa kawaida*,
kawia, ku-, v.i. delay, be late, dally.
kaya, n. members of a household.
kaza, ku-, v.t. fasten, tighten; *kaza kamba*, tighten a rope; *kaza mwendo*, move fast, kaza uzi, don't let go.
kazana, ku-, v.i. make efforts; *kazana vingine utafeli mtihani*, make efforts otherwise you'll fail your exams.
kazi, n. work, task, labour, *nguvu-kazi*, labour force, occupation, *fanya kazi*, do some work, *yuko kazini*, he is at work, *amekuja kikazi*, he is here on duty,.
kazia, ku-, v.t. fix on, *kazia macho*, fix the eyes on somebody or something 2. insist in something.
kazi-mradi, n. project, research work.
kebehi, ku-, v.t. abuse, offend.
kefu, adv. enough, *kula kefu yako*, eat your fill, see also **kifu**.
kejeli, ku-, v.t. mock.
kekee, n. brace and bit.
keketa, ku-, v.t. gnaw, cut away, *keketa wanawake*, circumcise women.
kelele, ma-, n. noise, *piga kelele*, make noise; *kelele!* quiet!
kemea, ku-, v.t. reprimand, scold.
kemeo, ma-, n. rebuke, scolding.
kemia, n. chemistry.
kemikali, n. chemicals.
kende, ma-, n. scrotum, testicles.
kengele, n. bell, *piga kengele*, ring a bell.

kengeza — kibao

kengeza, n. squint, *makengeza*, squinting eyes.
kera, ku-, v.t. bother, worry (cf kero).
kereka, ku-, v.i. be annoyed, be disappointed.
kerekta, ku-, v.i. prickle, irritate, vex.
kero, ma-, n. irritation, worry, annoyance, disappointment.
kesha, ku-, v.i. stay up all night 2. m-. n. a vigil.
keshi, n. cash.
keshia, ma-, n. cashier.
kesho, n. tomorrow, *kesho kutwa*, day after tomorrow.
kesi, n. case, *ana kesi*, he has a case.
kete, n. a pawn, small cowrie shell, *amekuzidi kete*, he has more pawns than you, he is in a stronger position.
keti, ku-, v.i. sit down.
ketisha, ku-, v.t. make somebody sit.
kiada, n. oderly, *vitabu vya kiada*, textbooks.
kiama, n. last day, judgement day.
kiambishi, n. affix, both prefix and suffix.
kiangazi, n. dry season.
kiapo, vi-, n. oath cf apa, *kula kiapo*, take an oath.
kiarabu, adj. arabic.
kiasi, n. amount, *kiasi gani?* how much? *kwa kiasi*, moderately, *ni mkubwa kiasi*, he is fairly big.
kiatu, vi-, n. shoe, *vaa viatu*, put on shoes, *vua viatu*, take off one's shoes.
kiazi, vi-, n. potato.
kibaka, vi-, n. pickpocket, petty thief.
kibakuli, vi-, n. small bowl.
kibali, vi-, n. permit, *ana kibali cha kazi*, he has a work permit, approval.
kibanda, vi-, n. hut, cottage.
kibaniko, vi-, n. roasting spit.
kibano, vi-, n. forceps.
kibanzi, vi-, n. splinter.
kibao, vi-, n. small board, slate 2. adv. meaning a large amount of

something, *watu kibao*, a lot of people 3. n. a slap, *piga kibao usoni*, give a slap on the face.

kibaraka, vi-, n. a vassal, puppet.

kibarua, vi-, n. casual worker, a day worker, *amepata kibarua*, he has obtained a casual job.

kibatari, vi-, n. small oil lamp.

kibeberu, adj. dictatorial, *serikali ya kibeberu*, an imperialist (dictatorial) government.

kibepari, adj. capitalist way.

kiberenge, vi-, n. small locomotive train 2. unmarried woman who runs after other women's men, *amekuwa kiberenge siku hizi*, she has become a prostitute these days.

kiberiti, see **kibiriti**.

kibindo, vi-, n. fold of the loin-cloth, *hamadi kibindoni*, a cry of luck when one picks up something.

kibiongo, vi-, n. hunchback.

kibiriti, vi-, n. match box, *washa kibiriti*, strike a match.

kibiritingoma, vi-, n. whore, prostitute.

kibla, n. imam's chamber in the mosque that he uses to lead prayers.

kibofu, vi-, n. urinary bladder.

kibogoyo, vi-, n. toothless person.

kiboko, vi-, n. hippo 2. whip made of hippo's hide, *chapa kiboko*, whip somebody.

kibonge, vi-, n. a fat person, something oversize.

kibua, vi-, n. tuna-like fish.

kibudu, vi-, n. carcass of an animal that was not slaughtered.

kiburi, n. arrogance, *fanya kiburi, onyesha kiburi*, be arrogant.

kiburudisho, vi-, n. refreshment, *ngoja tupate viburudisho hapa*, let's get some refreshments here.

kibuyu, vi-, n. calabash.

kibwengo   kidimbwi

kibwengo, vi-, n. sea devils, sea evil spirits.

kichaa, vi-, n. insanity 2. a mad person, *ana kichaa,* he is mad.

kichaga, vi-, n. construction for storing grain 2. Chaga language.

kichaka, vi-, n. bush(es).

kichane, vi-, n. bunch of fruit e.g. of bananas, grapes.

kicheche, vi-, skank, a stinking little animal like a cat.

kichefuchefu, n. nausea, sea sickness, *nasikia kichefuchefu,* I feel sick and want to vomit.

kichekesho, vi-, n. a funny situation, a comic theatrical work, comedy.

kicheko, vi-, n. laughter, *angua kicheko,* burst out laughing.

kichinichini, adv. secretively, fraudulently, underground movement.

kicho, vi-, n. fear, *ona kicho,* be timid.

kichocheo, vi-, n. what stirs up trouble, what stimulates trouble.

kichocho, vi-, n. bilharzia.

kichochoro, vi-, n. narrow passage, a small path.

kichogo, vi-, n. nape of the neck.

kichomi, vi-, n. sharp pain in the body, *ana kichomi,* he has sharp pains.

kichuguu, vi-, n. ant hill.

kichungi, vi-, n. cigarette filter.

kichwa, adv. headlong, *waligongana kichwa,* they collided headlong.

kichwa, vi-, n. head, *kichwa chini miguu juu,* upside down, *kichwa cha habari,* heading in a newspaper.

kidaka, vi-, n. early stages of coconut growth, coconut in that stage.

kidari, vi-, n. chest.

kidato, vi-, n. form I – VI of secondary school.

kidevu, vi-, n. chin, *ndevu,* beard, hair on the chin.

kidhi, ku-, v.t. satisfy, *kidhi shida zote,* meet all needs.

kidimbwi, vi-, n. pool, waterhole.

lifti   kifudifudi

lifti, adv. a little, *maji kidogo*, a little water, *kidogokidogo*, little by little.

kidokezi, vi-, n. anecdote.

kidokezo, vi-, n. hint, allusion, tip, clue, *kuna kidokezo chochote?* is there any hint?

kidole, vi-, n. finger.

kidole-tumbo, vi-, n. appendix.

kidomodomo, adj. talkative, *ana kidomodomo*, he talks too much.

kidonda, vi-, n. wound, ulcer.

kidonge, vi-, n. tablet, pill.

kidude, vi-, n. undefinable thing.

kidudu, vi-, n. small insect.

kiduva, ma-, n. hump.

kielekezo, vi-, n. sign, indicator.

kielelezo, vi-, n. illustration, graphic evidence.

kielezi, kielezo, vi-, n. adverb, *kielezi cha mahali*, adverb of place.

kienyeji, adv. traditional way, *fanya kienyeji*, do something without clear method, local.

kifaa, vi-, n. equipment, *vifaa vya shule*, school equipment.

kifaduro, vi-, n. whooping cough.

kifafa, vi-, n. epilepsy, *mwenye kifafa*, epileptic, *ana kifafa*, he is epileptic.

kifani, vi-, n. match, *haina kifani*, without match, unique.

kifaranga, vi-, n. chick.

kifaransa, n. French language.

kifaru, vi-, n. rhino 2. military tank.

kifo, vi-, n. death, *kufa*, to die.

kifu, ku-, v.t. satisfy, *chakula chako kimenikifu*, your food has satisfied me, see also **kefu**.

kifua, vi-, n. chest 2. cough, *hawezi kifua, ana kifua*, he coughs, has a flu.

kifudifudi, adv. on the face, *lala kifudifudi*, lie face down.

kifungo   kijani

kifungo, vi-, n. button, *funga kifungo*, button up 2. prison, *peleka kifungoni*, put in jail, a term in jail.

kifungu, vi-, n. section of an article.

kifunguakinywa, n. breakfast.

kifunguamimba, n. first born child.

kifuniko, vi-, n. cover.

kifupi, adv. briefly, adj. short, *kiti kifupi*, short chair.

kifusi, vi-, n. debris for construction.

kifuu, vi-, n. coconut shell.

kigae, vi-, n. tile (roof-tile).

kiganja, vi-, n. palm of the hand.

kigawanyo, vi-, n. division.

kigelegele, vi-, n. shout of joy, ululation.

kigeni, - a-, adj. foreign, *maneno ya kigeni*, foreign words, exotic.

kigeugeu, adj. fickle, caprice.

kigingi, vi-, n. stake, peg.

kigoda, vi-, n. local three legged stool.

kigoli, vi-, n. young girl just before puberty.

kigwena, n. conspiracy.

kiharusi, n. apoplexy, stroke, *anasumbuliwa na kiharusi*, he is suffering from stroke.

kihenge, vi-, n. barn.

kiherehere, n. too much anxiety, *ana kiherehere*, he is anxious.

kihisishi, vi-, n. interjection.

kihoro, vi-, n. anguish, deep grief.

kihusishi, vi-, n. preposition.

kiima, vi-, n. subject in a sentence.

kiingilio, vi-, n. fee to enable one enter.

kiini, vi-, n. kernel, essence, pith.

kiinimacho, vi-, n. magic, veilded truth, hynopsis.

kiinitete, vi-, n. embryo.

kiitikio, vi-, n. response, chorus.

kijakazi, vi-, n. slave girl.

kijana, vi-, n. youth.

kijani, adj. green, *shati la*

kijani, a green shirt.
kijasumu, vi-, n. bacterium, virus.
kijeraha, vi-, n. a small injury, a small sore.
kijicho, vi-, n. envy, *ana kijicho,* he is envious.
kijiji, vi-, n. village.
kijinga-moto, vi-, n. firebrand.
kijiti, vi-, n. twig.
kijito, vi-, n. stream, *kijito kimekauka,* a stream has dried up.
kijusi, vi-, n. foetus.
kikaango, vi-, n. frying pan.
kikao, vi-, n. sitting, meeting.
kikapu, vi-, n. basket.
kikasha, vi-, n. casket.
kike, adj. female, *mtoto wa kike,* a female child, girl.
kiko, vi-, n. smoking pipe, elbow (hand).
kikohozi, vi-, n. cough, *mwanangu anasumbuliwa na kikohozi,* my child is suffering from cough.
kikombe, vi-, n. cup, *kikombe cha chai,* a cup of tea, *kombe la dunia,* world cup.
kikomo-safari, n. destination.
kikonyo, vi-, n. stem that holds a fruit.
kikopo, vi-, n. can, tin.
kikosi, vi-, n. division in the military, a team of, brigade, unit, platoon, delegate.
kikundi, vi-, a small group, *kikundi cha wanafunzi,* a small group of students.
kila, adj. every, *kila mtu,* everybody.
Kilatini, n. Latin.
kilele, vi-, n. peak, climax, *Kilele cha Uhuru,* the Uhuru Peak.
kilema, vi-, n. handicapped person.
kilemba, vi-, n. turban, *vika mtu kilemba cha ukoka,* flatter somebody in order to deceive him
kilembwe, vi-, n. great-great grandchild, fourth generation.
kileo, vi-, n. intoxicant, liquor, alcohol.
kilima, vi-, n. hill.

kilimi, vi-, n. uvula.
kilimo, n. farming activity, agriculture.
kilio, vi-, n. mourning.
kilo, n. kilogramme.
kima, n. small monkey 2. minimum degree or amount e.g. *mshahara wa kima cha chini*, minimum wage.
kimachomacho, adv. openly, in public.
kimada, vi-, n. concubine, side mistress.
kimba, ma-, n. faeces.
kimbia, ku-, v.t. run, run away, flee, *walikimbia kutoka ukanda wa vita*, they fled from the war zone.
kimbilia, ku-, v.t. run to, after, *wamekimbilia sokoni*, they have run to the market (for protection).
kimbilio, ma-, n. refuge, assylum.
kimbiza, ku-, v.t. run after, chase.
kimbunga, vi-, n. hurricane, whirlwind.
kimelea, vi-, n. germ(s).
kimeng'enya, vi-, n. enzyme.

kimeta, n. anthrax.
kimo, vi-, n. height, size, *kimo cha mtu mzima*, the size of an adult person.
kimondo, vi-, n. meteor.
kimwana, vi-, n. beautiful girl.
kimya, n. silence, *kaa kimya*, do not speak, *kimya kingi kina mshindo mkuu* (prov), still waters
kina, n. depth 2. rhyme in poetry.
kinaganaga, kinagaubaga, adv. in detail, directly.
kinai, ku-, v.i. be satisfied, have more than enough.
kinaisha, ku-, v.t. satisfy fully, satiate; *nyama ya mafuta inakinaisha upesi*, fat meat satisfies easily.
kinakishi, vi-, n. computer see also **kompyuta**.
kinanda, vi-, n. piano, organ, *piga kinanda*, play an organ.
kinara, vi-, n. leader, *kinara wenu ni nani?* who is your leader?
kinasasauti, vi-, n. microphone.

kinda   kipazasauti

kinda, ma-, n. young, chick, child.
kinembe, vi-, clittoris.
kinena, vi-, n. groin.
kinga, v.t. protect 2. kinga, n. protection, *kinga ni bora kuliko tiba*, protection is better than cure.
kinu, vi-, n. mortar, mill.
kinubi, vi-, n. lyre, banjo.
kinyago, vi-, n. wood carving 2. despicable person.
kinyemi, vi-, n. something new, novelty, something that pleases the eye, beautiful.
kinyesi, vi-, n. excrement, faeces.
kinyonga, vi-, n. chameleon.
kinyongo, vi-, n. vendetta.
kinyozi, vi-, n. barber, du*ka la kinyozi*, barber's shop.
kinyume, vi-, n. the opposite.
kinywa, vi-, n. mouth.
kinywaji, vi-, n. drink, *utatumia kinywaji gani?* which drink will you take?

kioja, vi-, n. wonder, bugbear, something unusual.
kiongozi, vi-, n. leader, *kiongozi cha mwalimu*, teacher's guide.
kionyeshi, vi-, n. demonstrative, indicator.
kioo, vi-, n. glass, mirror.
kioski, vi-, n. kiosk.
kiota, vi-, n. nest.
kipaimara, n. sacrament of confirmation.
kipaji, vi-, n. talent, endowment, *mtu wa vipaji (akili) vingi*, a genius.
kipande, vi-, n. piece, part.
kipanga, vi-, n. falcon.
kipara, vi-, n. baldness.
kipato, vi-, n. income, profit, *kodi ya mapato*, income tax.
kipaumbele, vi-, n. priority, *kipaumbele chako ni kipi?* what is your priority?
kipawa, vi-, n. talent, intellectual gift, special capability.
kipazasauti, vi-, n. loud speaker.

85

kipengee   kisha

kipengee, vi-, n. detour.
kipengele, vi-, n. device, part of a document.
kipenyo, vi-, n. diameter, *nusu kipenyo*, radius.
kipeo, vi-, n. exponent, power in maths.
kipepeo, vi-, n. butterfly.
kipeuo, vi-, n. root of number.
kipigo, vi-, n. blow, stroke, *toa kipigo*, give a blow.
kipimajoto, vi-, n. thermometer.
kipimo, vi-, n. measurement.
kipindi, vi-, n. period, duration, a programme on radio or TV.
kipindupindu, n. cholera.
kipingamizi, vi-, n. obstacle.
kipofu, vi-, n. a blind person.
kipupwe, n. cold season, winter.
kipuri, vi-, n. spare part.
kipusa, vi-, n. tusk 2. girl (slang).
kirago, vi-, n. sleeping mat.
kiraka, vi-, n. cloth patch, fleck.

kirejeshi, vi-, n. reflexive pronoun.
kireno, n. Portuguese language.
kiri, ku-, v.t. confess, admit, *nakiri kupokea rushwa*, I confess having taken bribe.
kirimu, ku-, v.t. entertain, offer hospitality.
kiroboto, vi-, n. flea, insect.
kirukanjia, vi-, n. prostitute.
kirumi, n. Roman language, *Namba za Kirumi*, Roman Numbers.
kirungu, vi-, n. small club normally carried by policemen or militiamen or hunters.
kisa, vi-, n. episode 2. vendetta; *ana kisa nami*, he bears a grudge against me.
kisahani, vi-, n. saucer.
kisamvu, n. vegetable from cassava leaves.
kisanduku, vi-, n. small box.
kisha, adv. after that, thereafter.

kishada   kitambo

kishada, vi-, n. kite made of paper tied to a thread and let to fly in the sky being controlled by the thread.

kishawishi, vi-, n. temptation.

kishazi, vi-, n. clause.

kishenzi, adv. in a bad way, uncouthly.

kishikizo, vi-, n. button.

kishimo, vi-, n. dimple, *ana vishimo mashavuni mwake*, she has dimples on her cheeks.

kishindo, vi-, n. a loud sound; a sudden, loud noise.

kisi, ku-, v.t. kiss sb.

kisia, ku-, v.t. guess, infer.

kisifa, vi-, n. adjective see also **kivumishi**.

kisigino, vi-, n. heel, *kiatu cha kisigino kirefu*, high heeled shoes.

kisiki, vi-, n. tree stump.

kisima, vi-, n. well (of water).

kisimi, vi-, n. clitoris.

kisio, ma-, n. conjecture.

kisirani, vi-, n. bad omen, mishap 2. bad humour.

kisiwa, vi-, n. island, *kisiwa cha Pemba*, Pemba island.

kisogo, vi-, n. nape of the neck, *piga kisogo*, avoid.

kisoshalisti, n. socialistic, *nchi ya kisoshalisti*, socialistic country.

kisu, vi-, n. knife, *piga mtu kisu*, stab a person with a knife.

kisukari, n. diabetes.

kisukuku, vi-, n. fossil.

kisura, vi-, n. pretty girl.

kiswahili, n. Kiswahili language, *zungumza Kiswahili*, speak Kiswahili.

kitabu, vi-, n. book.

kitafunio, vi-, n. bite, snack.

kitako, vi-, n. butt, bicycle seat.

kitalu, vi-, n. nursery of a garden, seedbed for plants.

kitambaa, vi-, n. piece of cloth, rag.

kitambi, vi-, n. fat belly, beer belly; *ana kitambi*, he has a beer belly.

kitambo, vi-, n. period of time, *kitambo kidogo*, a little while, a short while.

kitambulisho   kiumbe

kitambulisho, vi. n. identity card, identificarion document.

kitana, vi-, n. comb.

kitanda, vi-, n. bed. *tandika kitanda*, make a bed, *kitanda - bembea.*, hammock.

kitangulizi, vi-, n. something that preceeds.

kitani, vi-, n. flax.

kitanzi, vi-, loop, noose.

kitasa, vi-, n. padlock, door locks.

kitendawili, vi-, n. riddle, dialemma.

kitendo, vi-, n. deed, action.

kitenge, vi-, n. wrapping cloth somehow heavier than kanga.

kitengo, vi-, n. section.

kitenzi, vi-, n. verb.

kiti, vi-, n. chair, *mwenyekiti, wenyeviti*, chairman, chairmen.

kitinda-mimba, vi-, n. last born child.

kitisho, vi-, n. bugbear, threat, *vitisho kutoka kwa magaidi*, threats from terrorists.

kitivo, vi-, n. faculty at a university.

kito, vi-, n. precious stone, *kito cha thamani*, gem.

kitongoji, vi-, n. part of a division/village.

kitovu, vi-, n. navel.

kitoweo, vi-, n. fish or meat for food.

kitu, vitu, n. thing; *si kitu*, it is nothing, it does not matter, *kitu gani hicho?* what is that thing?

kitubio, vi-, n. penance, repentance.

kitukuu, vi-, n. grandchild.

kitulizo, vi-, n. relief, consolation, *inanipa kitulizo*, it gives me consolation.

kitunguu, vi-, n. onion, *kitunguu saumu*, garlic.

kituo, vi-, n. stop, station, *Kituo cha Polisi Msimbazi*, Msimbazi Police Station, *kituo cha basi*, bus stop.

kiu, n. thirst; *ona kiu*, feel thirsty.

kiuka, ku-, v.t. transgress, overstep the limit.

kiumbe, vi-, n. creature, *viumbe hai*, living organisms, *elimu ya*

kiume   kizingiti

viumbe hai, biology.
kiume, adv. in a manly manner, brave.
kiunganishi, vi-, n. conjunction.
kiungo, vi-, n. spice, seasoning 2. part of body, copula 3. n. a go-between.
kiungulia, n. stomach acidity.
kiungwana, adv. gentlemanly, politely, *amekataa kiungwana*, he has refused politely.
kiuno, vi-, n. waist, cf *mgongo*, back, *mgongoni*, on the back.
kivuko, vi-, n. bridge, ferry.
kivuli, vi-, n. shadow, *kaa kivulini*, live in luxury.
kivumbi, adv. ado, in an excited manner.
kivumishi, vi-, n. adjective see also *kisifa*.
kivutio, vi-, n. incentive.
kiwa, adj. lonely.
kiwakilishi, vi-, n. pronoun.
kiwambo, vi-, n. diaphragm.
kiwanda, vi-, n. factory, industry.
kiwango, vi-, n. degree, level, standard, *kiwango cha juu*, high standard.
kiwanja, vi-, n. plot of land, stadium, open ground.
kiwembe, vi-, n. razor blade.
kiwete, vi-, n. lame, cripple.
kiwewe, n. state of confusion, *nimepatwa na kiwewe*, I'm confused.
kiwiko, vi-, n. elbow.
kiwiliwili, vi-, n. body.
kiyama, n. judgement day.
kiyeyusho, vi-, n. solvent.
kiyoyozi, vi-, n. air conditioner.
Kiyunani, n. Greek.
kizalia, vi-, n. offspring, defect inherited from one's ancestors.
kizazaa, vi-, n. confusion, caused by some misunderstandings.
kizazi, vi-, n, generation.
kizibo, vi-, n. cork, faucet.
kizimba, vi-, n. cage.
kizingiti, vi-, n. threshhold.

kiziwi   kompyuta

kiziwi, vi-, n. deaf person.
kizuio, kizuizi, vi-, n. obstruction, impediment.
kizuizi, vi-, n. detantion.
kizungu, adv. European-like, of western style.
kizunguzungu, n. dizziness.
klabu, vi-, n. club, bar.
kliniki, n. clinic.
kobe, n. tortoise, turtle.
koboa, ku-, v.t. to remove husks (rice, maize etc.), husk.
kocha, ma-, n. coach, trainer in sports.
kodi, n. tax, *toza kodi*, levy taxes, *lipa kodi*, pay taxes.
kodoa, ku-, v.t. open eyes wide, stare, *kodoa macho*, stare at.
kofi, ma-, n. clap, *piga makofi*, clap, ovation 2. slap, *kupiga kofi*, to slap.
kofia, n. cap, hat, *kofia ya chuma*, helmet.
kohoa, ku-, v.i. cough.
kohozi, ma-, n. cough.
kojoa, ku-, v.t. urinate, *kukojoa kitandani*, to wet a bed.
koka, ku-, v.t. kindle, *koka moto*, make fire.
kokota, ku-, v.t. drag, pull something behind oneself.
kokoto, n. pebble, grit.
koleo, ma-, n. pliers, shovel.
koma, ku-, v.i. stop, cease.
komaa, ku-, v.i. be ripe, mature.
komango, ma-, n. flint.
kombania, n. company, coy, squad (army).
kombe, ma-, big cup.
kombeo, ma-, n. sling.
kombo, ma-, n. crumbs, leftovers.
komboa, ku-, v.t. redeem, save, emancipate.
kombora, ma-, n. missile, bomb.
komea, ku-, v.i. end at 2. ku-, v.t. fasten with bolt.
komeo, n. bolt, *funga kwa komeo*, fasten with bolt.
komesha, ku-, v.t. stop, *komesha vita*, cease fire.
komoa, ku-, v.t. spoil somebody's plans, confuse.
kompyuta, n. computer,

komunyo

see also **kinakishi**.
komunyo, n. holy communion.
kona, n. corner, *kata kona*, turn.
konda, ku-, v. lose weight.
kondakta, ma-, n. conductor (bus).
konde, ma-, n. fist 2. farm in a valley.
kondesha, ku-, v.t. make sb thin.
kondoo, n. sheep.
kong'ota, ku-, v.t. hit by using sth.
kongamano, ma-, n. congress.
kongosho, n. pancreas.
konokono, n. snail.
konsonanti, n. consonant.
kontinenti, n. continent.
konyagi, n. Tanzanian whisky, gin.
konyeza, ku-, v.t. wink at, *alimkonyeza Asha*, he beckoned to Asha.
konyoa, ku-, v.t. tear off, pull off, *konyoa ndizi*, pull off bananas.
koo, ma-, n. throat 2. hen laying eggs.
kopa, ku-, v.t. borrow, take a loan.

kosefu

kopesha, ku-, v.t. lend, loan.
kopi, ku-, v.t. copy sth 2.n. copy, see also **nakala**.
kopo, ma-, n. can, tin.
koroboi, n. small oil lump.
korodani, n. testicles, scrotum.
korofi, adj. unruly, arrogant, rude, *ni mkorofi kama baba yake*, he is as rude as his father.
korofisha, ku-, v.t. spoil, detract.
koroga, ku-, v.t. stir, mix.
korokoro, n. dice gambling game.
korokoroni, n. detention, prison, guard.
koroma, ku-, v.i. snore, groan.
korosho, n. cashew nuts.
korti, n. court.
kosa, ma-, n. mistake, error 2. v. make a mistake 3. miss, *kosa shule*, miss school.
kosana, ku-, v.i. disagree with, quarrel.
kosefu, adj. faulty, sinful.

kosesha   kumbe

kosesha, ku-, v.t. lead astray, cause to make mistakes/miss.

kosoa, ku-, v.t. criticise.

kote, adv. everywhere.

koti, ma-, n. coat, *vaa koti*, put on a coat.

kovu, ma-, n. scar.

kozi, n. course, *chukua kozi ya Kiingereza*, take an English course.

krismasi, n. Christmas.

Kristo, n. Christ.

kua, ku-, v.i. grow, *mtoto anakua haraka*, the child is growing fast.

kubali, ku-, v.i. agree.

kubaliana, ku-, v.i. concur.

kubalika, ku-, v.i. be acceptable, agreeable.

kubalisha, ku-, v.t. convince, win over.

kubwa, adj. big, *mtu mkubwa*, big or a great person.

kucha, ma-, n. claw, fingernail.

kudra, n. divine gift, *kwa kudra ya Mola*, if God wills.

kufifia, v.i. flicker.

kufuli, n. padlock, *funga kwa kufuli*, lock with a padlock.

kufuru, ku-, v.i. blaspheme.

kuhani, ma-, n. priest, *kuhani mkuu*, high priest.

kuku, n. hen.

kule, adv. there, *kulekule*, there, on the spot.

kulia, adv. on the right hand. 2. v. to cry.

kuliko, adj. comparative, more than, *ni mrefu kuliko wewe*, he is taller than you.

kulikoni! interj. what's wrong?

kumba, ku-, v.i. suffer mishap, *amekumbwa na misiba*, misfortunes have overtaken him. 2. ku-, arrest indiscriminately, *polisi walitukumba wote*, police arrested us all indiscriminately.

kumbana na, ku-, v.i. encounter, come against.

kumbatia, ku-, v.t. embrace, fondle, *kumbatia mwanao*, fondle your son.

kumbe, interj. ah! is that so? sudden notice of something; *kumbe ni*

kumbo — kurupusha

wewe? so, it's you!
kumbo, ma-, n. push.
kumbuka, ku-, v.t. remember, *je, unanikumbuka?* do you remember me?
kumbukumbu, n. remembrance, comemoration.
kumbusha, ku-, v.t. remind, *unikumbushe baadaye,* remind me later.
kumbusho, ma-, museum, antiquities.
kumi, adj. ten.
kuna, existencial pron. there is, *kuna amani hapa,* there is peace here, there are 2. **ku-,** v.t. scratch.
kundi, ma-, n. group, crowd.
kung'fu, n. kung fu.
kung'uta, ku-, v.t. shake 2. beat badly.
kunguni, n. bed bug.
kunguru, n. crow.
kuni, n. firewood.
kunja, ku-, v.t. enfold, fold, *kunja uso,* frown.
kunjamana, ku-, v.i. be folded, have wrinkles.
kunjua, ku-, v.t. unfold, unroll.
kunradhi, interj. call to attention, *samahani,* pardon me, forgive me, excuse me.
kunyanzi, ma-, n. wrinkle, fold.
kupaa, n. ascension.
kupatwa-jua, n. solar eclipse.
kupatwa-mwezi, n. lunar eclipse.
kupe, n. tick, *usiwe kupe,* do not live at the expense of others.
kupita, adj. than, comperative degree, *Ali ni mrefu kupita Juma,* Ali is taller than Juma.
kuponi, n. coupon.
kupua, ku-, v.i. steal, take a big amount.
kupuo, m-, n. all at once, *nimefanya yote kwa mkupuo,* I have done all at once.
kura, n. vote, *piga kura,* cast votes.
kurugenzi, n. directorate.
kurupuka, ku-, v.i. run away frightened.
kurupusha, ku-, v.t. startle

kusanya   kwanza

kusanya, ku-, v.t. gather, collect, compile, congregate.

kusanyika, ku-, v.i. come together, assemble, congregate.

kushoto, adv. on the left-hand side.

kusini, n. south, in the south.

kusudi, n. purpose, *kwa makusudi,* purposely

kusudia, ku-, v.t. intend, *unakusudia kufanya nini?* what do you intend to do?

kusudio, ma-, n. intention, aim, purpose, objective.

kuta, n. pl. of ukuta, wall 2. ku-, v.t. find.

kutana, ku-, v.i. meet, *kutana na,* meet somebody, encounter somebody.

kuti, ma-, n. palm leaf.

kutu, n. rust, *shika kutu,* be rusty.

kuu, adj. great, superior, of high rank or position, *mwalimu mkuu,* headmaster, *Chuo Kikuu,* university.

kuukuu adj. old, worn out.

kuume, n. right, *mkono wa kuume,* right hand.

kuumeni, n. paternal side.

kuwadi, ma-, n. procurer.

kwa nini? inter. pron. why?

kwa, prep, to, for, by, *kwa mfano,* for instance.

kwaa, ku-, v.i. stumble over sth.

kwake, poss. pron. his, hers, *nyumba hii ni ya kwake,* this house is his/hers.

kwako, poss.pron. yours, *kosa hili ni la kwako,* this mistake is yours.

kwama, ku-, v.i. get stuck, find no way out.

kwamba, prep. in order that.

kwamisha, ku-, v. cause to get stuck, foil somebody's plans.

kwangu, possessive pron. mine, *kitabu hiki ni cha kwangu,* this book is mine, at my home, to me, as for me.

kwangua, ku-, v.t. scrape.

kwanza, adj. first, cf

kwao

kwanza, to begin with.
kwao, poss. pron. theirs, *kitabu hiki ni cha kwao*, this book is theirs, at their place.
kwapa, ma-, n. armpit.
kwapua, ku-, v.t. grab and snatch.
kwaresma, n. lent season.
kwaruza, ku-, v.t. scratch.
kwaruzana, ku-, v.t. quarrel with one another.
kwashiakoo, n. kwashiorkor, *ana kwashiakoo*, he/she has kwashiorkor.
kwata, n. drill, *cheza kwata*, drill.

kwinini

kwato, n. hoof.
kwatua, ku-, v.t. clean by removing, apply make ups to beautify oneself.
kwaya, n. choir.
kwea, ku-, v.t. climb up, ascend.
kweli, adj. true, *ni kweli*, it is true 2.adv. truly, certainly.
kwetu, poss. pron. ours, this house is ours, *nyumba hii ni ya kwetu* 2.adv. at ours.
kweza, ku-, v.t. exalt.
kwida, ku-, v.t. grab sb by the nake.
kwikwi, n. hiccup.
kwinini, n. quinine.

L

la!, interj. expression of surprise.

la, ku-, v.t. eat 2. adv. no, not at all.

laana, n. curse, *pata laana*, be cursed, damnation.

laani, ku-, v.t. to curse.

labda, adv. perhaps.

ladha, n. taste, flavour.

lafua, ku-, v.t. devour

lafudhi, n. accent, pronunciation, dialect, *una lafudhi ya kusini*, you have a southern accent.

laghai, adj. deceitful 2. **ku-**, v.t. cheat, cajole, falsify.

lahaja, n. dilect, *lahaja ya Kimtang'ata*, Kimtang'ata dialect of Swahili.

lahaula! interj. God forbid!

laini, adj. soft.

lainika, ku-, v.i. become soft.

lainisha, ku-, v.t. soften.

laiti, interj. would, that; *laiti angejua,* had he known.

lake, poss. pron. her, hers, his.

laki, adj. one hundred thousand 2. v. to go to meet somebody, *nenda ukamlaki dada yako*, go to meet your sister.

lakini, conj. but.

lakiri, n. sealing lead, seaing wax.

lako, poss. pron. your, yours, *shati lako*, your shirt.

lala, ku-, v.i. lie down, go to sleep.

lalama, lalamika, ku-, v.i. complain.

lalamiko, ma-, n. complaint, grievance, *toa malalamiko*, give complaints.

lalamiko, ma-, n. grievance.

lalana, ku-, v.t., copulate (sexually).

lalia, ku-, v.t. lie on.

lamba — letu

lamba, ku-, v.t. lick, see also **ramba**.
lamba, ku-, v.t. lick.
lami, n. tarmac, *barabara ya lami,* a tarmac road.
landana, ku-, v.t. look alike (mostly human beings).
lapa, ma-, n. sandal.
laumu, ku-, v.t. blame, reproach.
laumu, ku-, v.t. condemn.
lawama, n. blame, reproach.
lawiti, ku-, v.t. sodomize.
laza, ku-, v.t. lay down, put to sleep.
lazima, aux. v. must 2. u-, n. a must, necessity.
lazimika, ku-, v.i. be forced to, compel, *tumelazimika kuhama,* we have been compelled to shift.
lazimisha, ku-, v.t. force, compel.
lazimu, ku-, v.t. same as lazimisha
lea, ku-, v.t. rear, bring up, *mtoto umleavyo ndivyo akuavyo,* as you bring up a child so will it grow up.

lebo, n. label.
legea, ku-, v.i. be weak, languish.
legevu, adj. slack, weak.
legeza, ku-, v.t. unfasten, enervate, loosen, *legeza msimamo,* loosen one's stand.
leja, n ledger.
lemea, ku-, v.t. weigh heavily on somebody, oppress.
lenga, ku-, v.t. aim at.
lengalenga, v.i. be near crying, *machozi yalimlengalenga,* his eyes were tearful.
lengelenge, ma-, n. blister.
lengo, ma-, n. objective, aim.
leo, adv. to -day, *leoleo,* this very day.
lepe, n. light sleep.
leseni, n. licence, *leseni ya udereva,* driving licence.
leso, n. handkerchief.
leta, ku-, v.t. bring, *leta maji,* bring water.
letea, ku-, v.t. bring to, *ametuletea habari zote,* he has told us all about it.
letu, poss. pron. our, ours,

levi

jembe letu, our hoe.
levi, adj. drunken, *mtu mlevi*, a drunkard.
levya, ku-, v.t. intoxicate, *pombe inalevya*, alcohol intoxicates.
lewa, ku-, v.i. get drunk.
lewesha, ku-, v.t. make drunk, *pombe inalewesha*, alcoholic drinks intoxicate.
lia, ku-, v.i. cry, weep.
licha, conj. despite, *licha ya ushauri alifanya alivyotaka*, despite the advice he did as he wanted.
lifti, n. elevator, lift, *naomba lifti tafadhali*, can you give me a lift, please?
likizo, n. leave, vacation, holiday, *nipo likizo*, I'm on vacation.
lima, ku-, v.i. to cultivate, hoe, to till the land.
limau, ma-, n. lemon.
limbika, limbikiza, ku-, v.i. save up.
limbukeni, ma-, n. inexperienced at sth, novice.
limbuko, ma-, n. reserve, savings.

liwaza

linda, ku-, v.t. protect, defend.
lingana, ku-, v.i. be like or similar to.
linganifu, adj. what matches, symmetrical, following the same rules, comparative study.
linganisha, ku-, v.t. compare.
lini, adv. when? *utakuja lini?* when will you come?
lipa, ku-, v.t. pay.
lipiza, ku-, v.t. revenge, *lipiza kisasi*, avenge.
lipo, ma-, n. payment.
lipua, ku-, v.t. cause to explode.
lipuka, ku-, v.i. explode, *bomu limelipuka*, a bomb has exploded.
lisha, ku-, v.t. nourish, to feed.
lishe, n. nutritious food.
lita, n. litre.
litania, n. litany.
liturjia, n. liturgy.
livu, n. vacation.
liwali, ma-, n. magistrate.
liwaza, ku-, v.t. comfort sb, console, take out of a depressive mood.

liza

liza, ku-, v.t. cause to cry, *habari iliniliza*, the news made me cry.
lodi, ma-, n. well-to-do person, rich person.
lofa, ma-, n. poor person.
loga, ku-, v.t. bewitch.
longa, ku-, v.i. talk, say, *nilonge nisilonge?* should I say shouldn't I say?
losheni, n. lotion.
lowa, lowana, ku-, v.i. get wet.
lowanisha, ku-, v.t. make wet, put in water, soak with water.
lowea, ku-, v.i. settle, *mlowezi*, settler.
loweka, ku-, v.t. put something in water, soak in water.
lubega, n. style of dressing common among Maasai people.
lugha, n. language, *lugha ya kigeni*, foreign language.
lukuki, n. plentiful, many more than, a lot, *watu lukuki*, a lot of people.
lulu, n. pearl.
lumbana, ku-, v.t. debate, argue with one another.
lundikana, ku-, v.i. be crowed together, be piled up one on top of another.
lundo, ma-, n. heap, *lundo la nguo za mitumba*, a heap of second hand clothes.
luninga, n. television set, *tazama kipindi cha luninga*, watch at a TV programme, see also **televisheni**.
luteni, ma-, n. lieutenant (army).
luteni-jenerali, ma-, n. lieutenant general.
luteni-kanali, ma-, n. lieutenant-colonel.
luteni-usu, ma-, n. left-lieutenant/second lieutenant.
luva, n. louver.

M

maabara, n. laboratory.
maadili, n. moral requirements, ethical teachings, just conduct, edification.
maafa, n. disasters, mishaps, calamity, *maafa ya mafuriko*, floods disasters.
maafikiano, n. compromise, agreement.
maagizo, n. instructions, orders.
maajabu, n. wonders, *maajabu makubwa ya dunia*, great wonders of the world.
maalumu, adv. special, especially.
maamuma, n. blockhead, simpleton, illiterate.
maamuzi, n. decision, *fanya maamuzi sahihi*, make the right decisions.
maana, n. meaning, *maana yake nini?* what is the meaning?
maandalizi, n. prepartion.
maandamano, n. procession or demonstration, *walipanga maandamano makubwa*, they planned a big demonstration.
maandiko, n. writing, scripture, *maandiko matakatifu*, holy scripture.
maandishi, n. writing, scripture.
maangamizi, **maangamizo**, n. destruction, calamity, disaster, catastrophe.
maanisha, ku-, v.t. to mean, *unamaanisha nini?* what do you mean?
maarifa, n. experience, knowledge.
maarufu, adj. famous, well known.
maarusi, n. newly wed.
maasi, n. rebellion, *maasi yamemwondoa madarakani*, a rebellion has removed him from power.

mabadiliko

mabadiliko, n. changes, *mabadiliko ya hali ya hewa,* changes in wheather conditions.
mabaki, n. leftovers, remains, crumbs.
mabano, n. brackets.
mabaya, n. evil deeds, wickedness.
mabishano, n. arguments, controversy, disputes, *mabishano makubwa,* great disputes.
machachari, n. lacking in seriousness, superficial.
machafuko, n. storm, disorder, uprising, confusion.
macheche, n. trouble.
machela, n. stretcher.
macheo, n. sunrise.
machezo, n. witchcraft practices.
Machi, n. March.
machimbo, n. mines, quarring ground.
macho (sing. **jicho**), n. eyes.
machozi (sing. **chozi**), n. tears.
machungani, n. grazing land, pasture area/land.
machweo (*ya jua*), n. sunset.

maelezo

mada, n. topic of discussion.
madaha, n. elegance.
madai, n. claim, lawsuit, *madai yake dhidi ya serikali,* his claims against the government.
madaraka, n. authority, power of making decisions.
madhara, n. harm, damage.
madhehebu, n. denominations.
madhubuti, n. reliable, firm.
madhumuni, n. intention, aim.
madini, n. minerals, *Tanzania ni tajiri kwa madini,* Tanzania is rich in minerals.
madoadoa, n. spots, unsual signs on something, unwanted spots on clothes, etc.
madoido, n. embellishment.
madrasa, n. class, Quranic school.
maegesho, n. parking lot.
maelekeo, n. direction.
maelezo, n. explanation,

maendeleo   maiti

maelezo yako ni yapi? what is your explanation?

maendeleo, n. development, progress.

mafanikio, n. success.

maficho, n. hiding place.

mafindofindo, n. tonsils, tonsillitis.

mafua, n. colds, influenza, *anasumbuliwa na mafua*, he is suffering from cold.

mafundisho, n. teaching, lessons.

mafuriko, n. floods.

mafuta, n. oil, *mafuta ya taa*, kerosine (parafine), *mafutaghafi*, crude oil.

magendo, n. black marketing, illegal bussiness.

mageuzi, n. change.

magharibi, n. west.

magofu, n. deserted and destroyed building/house.

magongo, n. crutches.

magonjwa, n. diseases, *magonjwa ya kuambukiza,* contagious diseases.

magoti, n. knees, *piga magoti,* kneel down.

mahaba, n. love, romance, *wako kwenye mahaba makubwa,* they are engrossed in deep love.

mahabusu, n. prisoners, remand prison.

mahakama, n. court.

mahali, n. place, *hapa ni mahali pazuri*, this is a good place.

mahame, n. uninhabited old house, deserted place/building.

mahari, n. marriage settlement given by the husband to-be to the bride's family.

mahitaji, n. needs, wants, *mahitaji muhimu ya binadamu,* basic human needs.

mahojiano, n. interview.

mahubiri, n. homily, preaching, sermony.

mahususi, adj. special.

mahututi, adj. seriously ill, *ni mgonjwa mahututi*, he is very sick.

maili, n. mile.

maisha, n. life, living.

maiti, n. corpse, dead body.

majadiliano   malazi

majadiliano, n. discussion, dialogue.
majani, n. grass, tree leaves.
majaribu, n. trials, temptations, *majaribu ya shetani*, trials from the satan.
majeruhi, n. wounded (in battle or conflict), the injured.
maji, n. water, *majimaji*, watery.
majibishano, n. dialogue.
majira, n. season, *majira ya mvua*, rainy season.
majivuno, n. boast, *kuwa na majivuno*, be boastful.
majonzi, n. sorrow.
majuto, n. regret.
makaburi, n. graveyard, cemetery.
makala, paper, written presentation, news features.
makamu, n. vice-, *makamu wa rais*, vice-president.
makao, n. residence, *makao makuu*, headquarters.
makasi, mkasi, n. scissors.
makini, n. attention, *uwe makini sana*, be very attentive.
makofi, n. clap.
makombo, n. crumbs, leftovers.
makopa, n. dried cassava.
maksai, n. castrated bull, oxen.
maktaba, n. library, *maktaba kuu*, central library.
makubaliano, n. agreement, *makubaliano ya kusitisha mapigano*, ceasefire agreement.
makumbusho, n. meseum.
makundi, n. groups.
makusanyiko, n. gathering, assembly.
makusudi, adv. purposely, *kwa makusudi*, on purpose, intentionally.
makuzi, n. upbringing, child care.
malaika, n. angel, *malaika mlinzi*, guardian angel.
malaria, n. malaria.
malaya, n. prostitute, harlot, *amekuwa malaya*, she has become a prostitute.
malazi, n. place to sleep.

malezi, n. edification, *malezi ya kitawa*, religious formation.
mali, n. wealth, property, belongings.
malipo, n. payment, *malipo ya awali*, down payment.
maliwato, n. bathroom.
maliza, ku-, v.t. finish, complete.
malizika, ku-, v. be completed.
malkia, n. queen, *malkia wa uzuri*, queen of beauty.
malumbano, n. verbal argument.
mama, n. mother, *mama wa kambo*, step mother.
mamajusi, n. Magi.
mamantilie, n. food vendor.
mamba, n. crocodile.
mambo (sing. **jambo**), n. matter, issue, *mambo ya fedha*, financial matters.
mamboleo, n. modernity, new ways, *ukoloni mamboleo*, neo-colonialism.
mamia, n. hundreds, *mamia ya watu*, hundreds of people.
mamlaka, n. authority, power.
mamluki, n. mercenary.
mamoja, adv. the same, *ni mamoja kwake*, it is all the same to him.
manamba, n. migrant worker.
manane, n. *usiku wa manane*, deep in the night.
manati, n. slingshot.
mandari, n. picnic, *tunakwenda kwenye mandari*, we are going for a picnic.
manemane, n. myrrh.
maneno, n. words.
mang'amung'amu, n. consternation.
mang'amuzi, n. discerment, *pata mang'amuzi*, get discernment.
manifesto, n. manifesto, *manifesto ya kikomunisti*, communist manifesto.
manii, n. sperm, semen.
manispaa, n. municipality, *halmashauri ya manispaa*, municipal council.

manjano, n. yellow.
manowari, n. submarine, warship.
mantiki, n. logic, *kwa mantiki hii*, following this logic.
manufaa, n. advantage, utility, cf. *kufaa*, to be useful, benefit, *kwa manufaa yetu*, for our benefit.
manukato, n. perfume, fragrance.
manyunyu, n. drizzle.
maombi (sing. **ombi**), n. prayer, application, cf. *kuomba*, to pray for, beg.
maombolezo, n. mourning, weeping, cf *kuomboleza*, to mourn.
maongezi, n. talk, chat, cf. *kuongea*, to chat, talk.
maoni, n. viewpoint, cf. *ona*, see.
mapacha, n. twins.
mapambano, n. confrontation.
mapana, n. width.
mapatano, n. agreement.
mapato, n. income, *kodi ya mapato*, income tax.
mapema, adv. early.

mapendo (sing. **upendo**) n. love, affection.
mapenzi (sing. **penzi**) n. romantic love, affection, sense of caring for.
mapigano (sing. **pigano**), n. fight, battle.
mapinduzi, n. coup d'etat, revolution, *siku ya mapinduzi*, revolution day.
mapitio, n. review, *mapitio ya kitabu*, book review.
mapokezi, n. reception.
maporomoko, n. landslide, cascade, waterfalls.
mapumziko, n. rest, break.
mara, adv. times (x), *mbili mara mbili ni nne*, two times two equals four, suddenly.
maradhi, n. disease.
maradufu, adv. twice, double.
marahaba, n. answer to *shikamoo*.
marashi, n. nice scent from plants, *marashi ya karafuu*, clove scent/perfume.

marefu, n. length.
marehemu, n. the late so and so, deceased.
marekebisho, n. amendments, corrections.
maridadi, adj. well dressed, elegant, smart, *anaonekana maridadi*, he looks smart.
maridhiano, n. detente, *maridhiano ya kusini*, the south detente.
maringo, n. boast, arrogance, elegance.
marufuku, n. prohibition, *kupiga marufuku*, to prohibit, embargo.
marupurupu, n. fringe benefits.
masahihisho, n. correction.
mashairi, n. poems.
mashaka, n. great distress, worry.
mashambulizi, n. attack.
mashangilio, n. acclamation.
mashariki, n. east, *Afrika Mashariki*, East Africa.
mashimo (sing. **shimo**), n. holes.
mashindano, n. competition, match.
mashine, n. machine.
mashitaka (sing. **shitaka**), n. accusations, charges, complaints.
mashua, n. boat.
mashudu, n. dregs.
mashuhuri, adj. famous, *mtu mashuhuri*, famous person.
masihara, n. jest, fun.
masika, n. rainy season (in Tanzania between March and May).
masilahi, n. profit, gain.
masimbi, n. dregs, residue.
Masiya, n. Messiah, Christ.
masjala, n. registry.
maskani, n. home settlement, residence.
maskini, n. poor person, person of little or no income.
masomo, n. subjects, course of study.
masumbuko, n. , suffering, state of worry.
mataifa, nations.
matako, n. buttocs, bum.
matakwa, n. wishes, needs, *matakwa yako ni yapi?* what are your

matanga   maziara

wishes?
matanga, n. place of mourning, period of mourning.
matarumbeta, n. trumpets.
matata, n. trouble.
matayarisho, n. preparation.
mate, n. saliva.
matege, n. rickets, bowlegs.
mateka, n. war prisoner, booty.
matembezi, n. excursion, walk, *matembezi ya hiari*, charity walk.
matengenezo, n. maintanance, repair, rehabilitation, renovation.
mateso, n. suffering, pain.
mateto, n. criticism.
mathalani, adv. for instance.
matibabu, n. treatment (medical).
matiti, n. breasts, teats.
matokeo, n. results.
matumaini, n. hope.
matumbo, n. bowels.
matumizi, n. uses, expenditure, consumption, *ni nzuri kwa matumizi ya binadamu*, good for human consumption.
matusi, n. insults, *matusi ya nguoni*, insults on the genitaria.
maua, n. flowers.
mauji, n. massacre, *mauji ya halaiki*, genocide.
Maulidi, n. Prophet Mohammed's birthday.
maulizo, n. inquiries.
maumbile, n. nature, physical make up, morphology.
maumivu, n. pain, suffering.
maungo, n. limbs.
mauti, n. death.
mauzo, n. marketing.
mavazi (sing. **vazi**) n. dress(es).
mavi, n. dung, excrement, feaces.
mavuno, n. harvest, crop, yield.
mawasiliano, n. communication, *njia za mawasiliano*, means of communication.
mawio, n. (*ya jua*) sunrise.
mazao, n. crop, produce.
maziara, n. cemetery.

maziko, n. burial.
mazingaombwe, n. illusory tricks, magic.
mazingara, n. superstition.
mazingira, n. environment, *mazingira mazuri ya biashara*, good business environment.
mazishi, n. burial, funeral.
maziwa, n. milk, breasts, *nyonyesha mtoto maziwa*, suckle the baby.
mazoea, n. habit, custom.
mazoezi, n. physical exercises, class assignments.
mazungumzo, n. talk, chat, *mazungumzo ya amani*, peace talks.
mba, n. dandruff.
mbaazi, n. pigeon peas.
mbaguzi, wabaguzi, n. racist(s), those who practice discrimination.
mbalamwezi, n. moonlight at its brightest.
mbali, adv. far off, *kaa mbali*, stay away, at a long distance.
mbalimbali, adj. apart, *wanaishi mbalimbali*, they live apart, different, *vitu mbalimbali*, different things.
mbavu (sing. **ubavu**), n. ribs, *wa ubavu wangu*, my better half.
mbawa (sing. **ubawa**), n. wings.
mbege, n. finger millet, Chaga local brew.
mbegu, n. seeds, *mbegu za miti*, trees seeds.
mbele, prep. in front, *mbele ya shule*, in front of a school.
mbelewele, n. pollen.
mbili, adj. two,
mbilikimo, n. pygmy.
mbinguni, n. heaven.
mbinu, n. strategy, strategies, tactics.
mbio, n. speed, *nenda mbio*, run.
mbishi, wa-, n. disputant, adj. argumentative.
mbiu, n. proclamation, *mbiu ya pasaka*, the Easter Proclamation.
mbizi, n. dive, *kupiga mbizi*, to dive.
mboga, n. vegetable(s).
mbogo, n. buffalo.
mbolea, n. manure, fertilizer.

**mbona, **interrog. why?
**mboni, **n. eyeball.
**mboo, **n. penis, see also uboo, mbolo.
**mbu, **n. mosquito.
**mbuga, **n. plains, national parks, *je, umewahi kwenda kwenye mbuga?* have you ever been to a national park?.
**mbung'o, **n. tsetse fly.
**mbunge, wa-, **n. Member of Parliament.
**mbuni, **n. ostrich.
**mbuyu, **n. baobab tree.
**mbuzi, **n. goat.
**mbwa, **n. dog, *mbwamwitu,*wolf, jackal.
**mbweha, **n. fox.
**mbwembwe, **n. elegance (walking style).
**mchakao, **n. deterioration.
**mchakato, mi-, **n. process, *michakato ya kiakili,* mental processes.
**mchambuzi, **n. analyst.
**mchana, **n. day-time.
**mchanga, **n. sand adj. very young, *mtoto mchanga,* baby.
**mchanganuo, **n. analysis.
**mchanganyiko, **n. mixture.

**mchango, mi-, **n. collection, contribution.
**mchapaji, wa-, **n. printer.
**mchapishaji, wa-, **n. publisher.
**mchapo, mi-, **n. blow (fig.) saucy story, tale, gossip, a chat, *Ana kwa michapo!* Ann is so good at chatting!
**mchawi, wa-, **n. witch.
**mche, mi-, **n. seedling, shoot.
**mchecheto, **n. panic.
**mchekeshaji, **n. comedian.
**mchele, **n. rice (uncooked), *wali,* cooked rice.
**mchenza, **n. tangerine tree.
**mcheshi, wa-, **n. clown, jester, charming, cheerful.
**mchezaji, wa-, **n. player.
**mchezo, mi-, **n. play, game.
**mchi, mi-, **n. pestle.
**mchicha, **n. a vegetable like spinnach.
**mchinjaji, wa-, **n. slaughterer.
**mchirizi, mi-, **n. gutter.
**mchokozi, wa-, **n. teaser,

mchongaji — mema

trouble-maker, an aggressor.
mchongaji, wa-, n. carver.
mchoraji, wa-, n. artist, cartoonist, illustrator, designer.
mchoro, mi-, n. sketch, drawing, illustration.
mchoroko, mi-, n. green gram plant.
mchoyo, adj. miser, greed.
mchukuzi, wa-, n. coolie, bearer.
mchumba, wa-, n. fiancee, sweetheart, *tafadhali kutana na mchumba wangu*, please meet my fiancee.
mchungaji, wa-, n. pastor, herder, pastoralist.
mchunguzi, wa-, n. reseacher, investigator.
mchungwa, mi-, n. orange tree.
mchuuzi, wa-, n. retailer, vendor.
mchuzi, mi-, n. soup, gravy.
mchwa, n. white ants.
mdahalo, mi-, n. public debate, *shiriki kwenye mdahalo*, participate in a public debate.
mdai, wa-, n. creditor.
mdanganyifu, wa-, n. liar, fraud, cheat, see also tapeli.
mdeni, wa-, n. debtor.
mdhamini, wa-, n. bailsman, sponsor.
mdokozi, wa-, n. petty thief.
mdomo, mi-, n. mouth, lip.
mdudu, wa-, n. insect.
mdundiko, n. Zaramo traditional dance.
mdundo, mi-, n. beat in music, rhythm.
mea, ku-, v.i. grow, germinate.
mechi, n. match.
medali, n. medal, *medali ya dhahabu*, gold medal.
medani, n. arena, fighting ground.
mega, ku-, v.t. break a piece off something.
megawati, n. megawatt.
Mei, n. May.
meja, n. major (rank in the army).
meli, n. ship.
mema, n. good acts, *tenda mema*, perform good deeds.

mende

mende, n. cockroach.
menejimenti, n. management.
meno, n. teeth (jino, tooth).
menya, ku-, v.t. peel off.
meremeta, ku-, v.i. shine brightly.
mesenja, ma-, n. messenger.
methali, n. proverb, also mithali.
meya, ma-, n. mayer, *Meya wa Manispaa,* Mayer of a Municipality.
meza, ku-, v.t. swallow.
meza, n. table, *mezani,* at, on the table.
mezea, ku-, v.i. (fig.), forgive and forget 2. use some liquid to swallow something.
mfadhaiko, n. depression.
mfadhili, wa-, n. sponsor, benefactor, donor, *nchi fadhili,* donor contries.
mfagiaji, wa-, n. sweeper.
mfagio, mi-, n. broom.
mfalme, wa-, n. king, ruler, chief.
mfano, mi-, n. example, *kwa mfano,* for example, *toa mfano,* give an example.
mfanyabiashara, wa-, n. businessman/woman, trader.
mfanyakazi, wa-, n. worker, a salaried person, *mimi ni mfanyakazi,* I'm a worker.
mfarakano, mi-, n. cleavage.
mfariji, wa-, n. consoler.
mfawidhi, wa-, n. master of (ceremony/food distribution).
mfenesi, mi-, n. jackfruit tree.
mfereji, mi-, n. stream, drain.
mfigili, mi-, n. radish plant.
mfiraji, wa-, n. sodomite.
mfiwa, wa-, n. bereaved person.
mfuachuma, wa-, n. blacksmith.
mfuasi, wa-, n. follower, disciple.
mfuatano, mi-, n. concord.
mfugo, mi-, n. domestic animal, goat, cattle, sheep.

mfungo

mfuko, mi-, n. bag, pocket.
mfululizo, mi-, n. succession, series.
mfumo, mi-, n. system, mode, *mfumo wa uzalishaji*, mode of production, *mfumo wa hewa*, respiratory system.
mfungo, n. fast.
mfungwa, wa-, n. prisoner, captive.
mfuniko, mi-, n. cover, lid.
mfupa, mi-, n. bone.
mfuria, wa-, n. friar.
mfyatuko, mi-, n. a sudden release of sth.
mgahawa, mi-, n. coffee shop, canteen, restaurant, internet cafe.
mgambo, n. proclamation 2. militia, *la mgambo likilia kuna jambo*, when a proclamation is made there is something important (prov.).
mganda, n. a traditional dance from one of the southern regions of Tanzania 2. n. Ugandan.
mganga, wa-, n. doctor, medicine man.
mgao, mi-, n. division, rationing, *mgao wa umeme*, power rationing.
mgawaji, wa-, n. distributor.
mgawanyiko, mi-, n. division, partition.
mgeni, wa-, n. guest, visitor.
mgombea, wa-, n. election candidate.
mgomo, mi-, n. strike.
mgomvi, wa-, n. quarrelsome person, an aggressor.
mgongano, mi-, n. clash, collision.
mgongo, mi-, n. back.
mgoni, wa-, n. adulterer.
mgonjwa, wa-, n. patient, sick person.
mgumba, wa-, n. childless person (person not capable of getting children).
mguno, mi-, n. grumbling.
mguu, mi-, n. leg, foot.
mhadhara, mi-, n. public discourse/lecture.
mhadhiri, wa-, n. lecturer.
mhaini, wa-, n. traitor, betrayer.

mhakiki — mimba

mhakiki, wa-, n. critic, reviewer.
mhalifu, wa-, n. criminal, offender.
mhamiaji, wa-, n. immigrant.
mhandisi, wa-, n. contractor, engineer.
mhanga, wa-, n. victim(s), *wahanga wa vita vya kienyeji*, victims of civil war, see also **kafara**.
mharibifu, wa-, n. destructive person.
mhariri, wa-, n. editor.
mhasibu, wa-, n. accountant, *mhasibu mkuu*, chief accountant.
mhazili, wa-, n. office secretary.
mhemuko, mi-, n. emotion.
mheshimiwa, wa-, n. Honourable, Her/His Excellency.
mhimili, n. axis.
mhindi, mi-, n. maize plant, **Mhindi**, wa-, n. Indian.
mhisani, wa-, n. benefactor.
mhubiri, wa-, n. preacher, homilist, sermonist.
mhujumu, wa-, n. saboteur.
mhuni, wa-, n. hooligan.
mhuri, mi-, n. stamp, *piga mhuri*, to stamp with official stamp or seal.
mia, adj. hundred, *watu mia nne*, four hundred people.
miayo, pl. n. yawn; *piga miayo*, yawn.
mifugo, n. livestock.
mila, n. custom, tradition.
milele, n. eternity 2. adv. eternally, *milele na milele*, for ever and ever.
milia, n. stripe, *pundamilia*, zebra.
miligramu, n. milligram.
miliki, ku-, v.t. possess, *kampuni inamilikiwa na wafanyakazi*, the company is owned by workers 2. n. possession, *hii ni miliki yangu*, this is my possession.
milimita, n. milimetre.
milionea, ma-, n. millionaire.
milioni, adj. million.
mimba, n. pregnancy, *pata, tunga, chukua, shika mimba*, become

mimi   mkabala

pregnant; *tia mimba*, pregnant woman.
mimi, pron. I; *mimi mwenyewe*; I myself.
mimina, ku-, v.t. pour.
miminika, ku-, v.i. pour out.
minya, squeeze.
minyoo, n. worm.
miongoni, prep. among, *miongoni mwa watu*, among the people.
mirathi, n. inheritance.
misa, n. a liturgical service for Christians, especially, Catholics.
misale, n. missal.
mita, n. miter.
mithali, n. proverb, also methali.
mitindo, n. styles.
mitishamba, n. herbal medicine, *mtaalamu wa mitishamba*, herbalist.
miwani, n. spectacles, glasses, *miwani ya jua*, sun goggles.
mizani, n. weighing scale.
mizigo, n. baggage.
mja, wa-, n. human being, *Mungu hamtupi mja wake*, God does not abandon the person he created, *mja mzito*, a pregnant woman.
mjadala, mi-, n. discussion between opponents.
mjakazi, wa-, n. female slave/servant.
mjamzito, wa-, n. pregnant woman.
mjane, wa-, n. widow, widower.
mjanja, wa-, n. clever person.
Mjerumani, wa-, n. German.
mji, mi-, n. town, city, an urban area.
mjinga, wa-, n. fool, stupid, clod.
mjomba, wa-, n. uncle (mother's brother), *je, mjomba wako anakuja nawe?* is your uncle coming with you?.
mjukuu, wa-, n. grandchild.
mjumbe, wa-, n. deputed person, delegate, envoy.
mjusi, mi-, lizard.
mkaa, n. charcoal; *jipalia mkaa*, get oneself in trouble.
mkabala, n. opposite, *mkabala na Kanisa la Zamani*, opposite the

Old Church.
mkaguzi, wa-, n. inspector, *mkaguzi wa mahesabu,* auditor.
mkahawa, mi-, n. coffee tree.
mkaidi, wa-, n. stubborn person, headstrong.
mkakati, mi-, n. strategy, plan.
mkalimani, wa-, n. interpreter, translator.
mkanda, mi-, n. belt.
mkandamizaji, wa-, n. oppressor, dictator.
mkanganyiko, mi-, n. confussion.
mkano, n. denial, *mkano binafsi,* self denial.
mkaratusi, mi-, n. eucalyptus.
mkasa, mi-, n. unpleasant event, scandal, *mkasa wa Monica Lewinsky,* the Monica Lewinsky scandal.
mkasi, mi-, n. pair of scissors.
mkataba, mi-, n. contract; *fanya mkataba,* make a contract.
mkate, mi-, n. bread, *oka mikate,* bake bread; *mwoka mikate,* baker.
mkato, mi-, n. comma, (/) 2. act of cutting.
mkazo, n. emphasis.
mke, wake, n. wife (wives); *chukua mke,* marry a wife; *acha mke,* divorce a wife.
mkebe, mi-, n. can.
mkeka, mi-, n. mat; *suka mkeka,* weave a mat.
mkesha, mi-, n. vigil, eve, *mkesha wa mwaka mpya,* new year eve.
mkia, mi-, n. tail, *fyata mkia,* show fear.
mkimbizi, wa-, n. refugee, *mtoro mkimbizi,* fugitive.
mkinzani, wa-, n. opposer.
mkoba, mi-, n. bag, wallet, parcel, handbag, briefcase, *mkoba umeibiwa,* a bag has been stolen.
mkojo, mi-, n. urine.
mkokoteni, mi-, n. push-cart.
mkoloni, wa-, n. colonialist.
mkoma, wa-, n. leper, **ukoma,** n. leprosy.
mkomamanga, mi-, n. pomegranate.

mkombozi — mlalamishi

mkombozi, wa-, n. saviour, liberator, redeemer.
mkondo, mi-, n. current, rush.
mkonga, mi-, n. trunk of an elephant.
mkonge, mi-, n. sisal, also **katani**.
mkongojo, mi-, n. crutch.
mkono, mi-, n. hand, arm; *pokea kwa mikono miwili*, receive with open arms.
mkopo, mi-, n. loan, credit, *pata mkopo wa benki*, get a bank loan.
mkora, wa-, n. hooligan, rascal.
mkorofi, wa-, n. troublesome person, arrogant.
mkufu, mi-, n. chain.
mkuki, mi-, n. spear.
mkulima, wa-, n. farmer, peasant.
mkumbo, mi-, n. shove, push.
mkundu, mi-, n. anus.
mkunga, wa-, n. midwife.
mkungu, mi-, n. a bunch of bananas.
mkupuo, mi-, n. knocking something off in one go, *alikunywa kikombe cha chai kwa mkupuo*, he drank the whole cup in one gulp.
mkurugenzi, wa-, n. director, *mkurugenzi mtendaji*, managing director.
mkusanyiko, mi-, n. gathering.
mkutano, mi-, n. meeting, *fanya mkutano;* hold a meeting, congress.
mkutubi, wa-, n. librarian.
mkuu, wa-, n. person in charge, leader, boss.
mkuyu, mi-, n. wild fig tree.
mkware, wa-, n. sex maniac, lascivious.
mkwe, wa-, n. in-law(s).
mkweche, mi-, n. old car/bicycle/motorcycle.
mkwezi, wa-, n. climber.
mkwiji, mi-, n. girdle.
mlafi, wa-, n. glutton, *yeye ni mlafi*, he is a glutton.
mlaghai, wa-, n. a cheat, adj. deceitful.
mlalamishi, wa-, n. complainant.

mlango   mnamo

mlango, mi-, n. door; *mlangoni*, at the door, doorway.
mlanguzi, wa-, n. black marketeer.
mlawiti, wa-, n. sodomite, see also **mfiraji**.
mlei, wa-, n. layman.
mlemavu, wa-, n. disabled person.
mlevi, wa-, n. drunkard.
mlezi, wa-, n. one who brings up a child, guardian.
mlima, mi-, n. mountain, *Mlima Kilimanjaro*, Mount Kilimanjaro.
mlimau, mi-, n. lemon tree.
mlimbwende, wa-, n. beautiful girl(s), stylish.
mlingoti, n. gallows.
mlinzi, wa-, n. guardian, watchman, custodian, *mlinzi wa nchi/ardhi*, custodian of the land.
mlio, mi-, n. cry, shout.
mlipaji, wa-, n. payer.
mlipwaji, wa-, n. payee.
mlo, mi-, n. food.
mlokole, wa-, n. neophyte, born again christian.

mlowezi, wa-, n. settler, immigrant.
mlundikano, mi-, n. heap, congestion.
mlungula, mi-, n. bribe.
mluzi, mi-, n. whistle by mouth.
mmachinga, wa-, n. hawker (street language, not official).
Mmarekani, wa-, n. American.
mmbea, wa-, n. gossiper, scandalmonger.
mmea, mi-, n. plant.
mmeng'enyo, mi-, n. digestion process.
mmilikaji, wa-, n. property owner.
mmomonyoko, mi-, n. erosion, decadence, *mmomonyoko wa maadili*, moral decadence.
mnada, mi-, n. auction.
mnadhimu mkuu, wa-, n. chief of staff.
mnafiki, wa-, n. hypocrite, impostor, kauleni.
mnajimu, wa-, n. astronomer.
mnamo, adv. about, *mnamo saa moja*

asubuhi, about 7 a.m.
mnanasi, mi-, n. pineaple plant, *kilimo cha minanasi*, pineaple cultivation.
mnara, mi-, n. tower, *mnara wa Babeli*, the tower of Babel 2.n. *mnara wa sabuni*, bar of soap.
mnato, mi-, n. adhesion.
mnazi, mi-, n. coconut tree, palm tree.
mneso, mi-, n. flexibility.
mninga, mi-, n. African teak, bloodwood.
mno, adv. very much, too much of.
mnofu, mi-, n. flesh, meat, steak.
mnong'ono, mi-, n. whispering, rumours, *hii ni minong'ono tu*, these are mere rumours.
mnung'unikaji, wa-, n. discontented person.
mnunuzi, wa-, n. buyer, customer, also see **mteja, wa-,** n. customer, client.
mnururisho, mi-, n. radiation.
mnyakuzi, wa-, n. snatcher.

mnyama, wa-, n. animal, beast.
mnyang'anyi, wa-, n. robber, bandit.
mnyapara, wa-, n. overseer, foreman.
mnyenyekevu, wa-, n. humble person.
mnyoo, mi-, n. worm.
mnyororo, mi-, n. chain, fetter.
modeli, n. model.
mofimu, n. morpheme.
moja, adj. one; *mojamoja*, one by one; *moja kwa moja*, straight on.
mola, n. God, Lord, Allah.
momonyoka, ku-, v.i. be eroded, crumble away, *kumomonyoka kwa maadili*, moral decadance.
morali, n. morale, enthusiasm.
mori, n. zeal, eagerness, enthusiasm, state of intense fury leading to foaming in the mouth and loss of self control.
moshi, mi-, n. smoke.
mosi, adj. first, *Mei Mosi*, first day of the month of

motisha

May, International Labour Day.
motisha, n. motivation, promotion.
moto, n. fire, *washa moto*, start a fire, *zima moto*, put off a fire.
moyo, mi-, n. pl. mioyo (**nyoyo**), heart(s).
mpagani, wa-, n. pagan, heathen, *kafiri*, non-believer.
mpagazi, wa-, n. porter.
mpaji, wa-, n. benefactor, provider, giver, see also **mhisani**, **mfadhili**.
mpaka, mi-, n. boundary 2. prep. until; *hapa mpaka pale*, from here to there.
mpako, mi-, n. coating, anointment, *sakramenti ya mpako mtakatifu*, sacrament of holy anointment.
mpambaji, wa-, n. decorator.
mpambe, wa-, n. aide-camp, bodyguard, bestman/bridesmaid.
mpando, n. ascension.
mpangaji, wa-, n. tenant.
mpango, mi-, n. plan, order.

mpotovu

mparachichi, mi-, n. avocado tree.
mpasuko, mi, n. cleavage, disruption.
mpatanishi, wa-, n. arbitrator.
mpelelezi, wa-, n. spy, inquirer.
mpembuzi, wa-, n. analyst.
mpendwa, wa-, n. beloved one, *kwa mpendwa wangu*, to my beloved.
mpera, mi-, n. guava tree.
mpiganaji, wa-, n. fighter.
mpigataipu, n. typist.
mpingo, mi-, n. ebony tree.
mpini, mi-, n. handle.
mpinzani, wa-, n. (political) opponent.
mpira, mi-, n. ball 2. rubber.
mpishi, wa-, n. cook, *tumepata mpishi mpya*, we have got a new cook.
mpito, n. transition.
mpokeaji, wa-, n. receiver, recipient, receptionist.
mpotevu, wa-, n. prodigal, *mwana mpotevu*, prodigal son.
mpotovu, wa-, n. heretic,

see also, **muasi-dini**.
Mprotestanti, wa-, n. Protestant.
mpumbavu, wa-, n. fool, *usiwe mpumbavu*, don't be a fool.
mpwa, wa-, n. niece (female), nephew (male).
mraba, mi-, n. square, row.
mrabaha, n. a share in business, royalty.
mradi, mi-, n. project 2. adv. provided.
mrembo, wa-, n. pretty woman.
mrithi, wa-, n. interitor, heir.
mroho, wa-, n. greedy.
msaada, mi-, n. help, assistance, aid.
msafara, mi-, n. convoy.
msafiri, wa-, n. traveller.
msagaji, wa-, n. lesbian.
msaidizi, wa-, n. assistant, deputy, second in rank, aide.
msajili, wa-, n. registrar.
msako, mi-, n. search, hunt.
msalaba, mi-, n. cross, crucifix.
msaliti, wa-, n. traitor, betrayer.

msalkheri, interj. good evening.
msamaha, mi-, n. pardon, forgiveness, amnesty, *msamaha wa Rais*, Presidential amnesty.
msamiati, mi-, n. vocabulary, lexicon.
msanifu, wa-, n. designer, *msanifu wa ramani*, map designer.
msanii, wa-, n. artist.
msaragambo, mi-, n. volunteer work, also **harambee**.
msarifu, n. bursar.
msasa, mi-, n. emery paper.
mseja, wa-, n. celibant, unmarried person for special aim (religious).
msemaji, wa-, n. speaker, spokesman/woman.
mseminari, wa-, seminarian (s), *mseminari wa zamani*, ex-seminarian.
msemo, mi-, n. saying.
msengenyaji, wa-, n. backbiter.
mseto, n. mixture, coalition, *serikali ya mseto*, coalition government.

mshahara — msingi

mshahara, mi-, n. wage, pay, salary.
mshairi, wa-, n. poet, *mshairi mashuhuri,* a fomous poet.
mshale, mi-, n. arrow, hand(s) of a clock.
mshangao, mi-, n. wonder, surprise.
mshauri, wa-, n. adviser, counsellor.
mshawishi, wa-, n. persuader, seducer.
mshenga, wa-, n. a go-between in arranging a marriage.
mshenzi, wa-, n. ill-mannered person, uncouth.
mshikaji, wa-, n. a man who keeps a woman as mistress.
mshikaki, mi-, n. grilled pieces of meat on a wire, shish kebab.
mshikamano, mi-, n. cohesion, togetherness.
mshindani, wa-, n. competitor, rival, opponent.
mshindi, wa-, n. winner, *mshindi wa leo,* today's winner.
mshindo, n. boom (commerce), orgasm (sexual intercourse).
mshipa, mi-, n. blood vessel.
mshipi, mi-, n. cincture.
mshirika, wa-, n. partner, associate.
mshtakiwa, wa-, n. accused, defendant.
mshtuko, mi-, n. shock.
mshumaa, mi-, n. candle, *mwangaza wa mshumaa,* candle light.
mshupavu, wa-, n. fearless person, courageous, strong.
msiba, mi-, n. calamity, disaster, bereavement.
msichana, wa-, n. girl, *msichana mrembo,* a beautiful girl.
msikilizaji, wa-, n. listener.
msikiti, mi-, n. mosque.
msimamizi, wa-, n. supervisor, overseer, warden.
msimu, mi-, n. season.
msimulizi, wa-, n. narrator.
msingi, mi-, n. foundation, basis.

msiri, wa-, n. confidant.
msisimko, mi-, n. excitement, *msisimko mkubwa*, a great excitement.
msitu, mi-, n. forest.
msokoto, mi-, n. twisting, weaving.
msomeshaji, wa-, n. teacher, one who sponsors anothers education.
msomi, wa-, n. elite, intellectual, *wasomi wa Afrika*, African intellectuals.
msongano, msongamano, mi-, n. crowding, multitude, congestion.
msonge, mi-, n. circular house in the pyramidal shape, hierarchy.
mstaafu, wa-, n. retired person.
mstaarabu, wa-, n. civilised person, gentleman/respectable lady.
mstahiki, wa-, n. deserving special respect.
mstari, mi-, n. line, *piga mstari*, draw a line.
mstatili, n. rectangle.

msukosuko, mi-, n. turmoil, agitation.
msukumo, n. pressure, impulse.
msuluhishi, wa-, n. mediator, *msuluhishi katika mazungumzo ya amani*, mediator in the peace talks.
msumari, mi-, n. nail.
msumbufu, wa-, n. a nuisance., a troublesome person.
msumeno, mi-, n. saw.
mswaki, mi-, n. toothbrush.
mtaa, mi-, n. quarter, locality in the city, street.
mtaalamu, wa-, n. expert, *wataalamu wa kigeni*, foreign experts.
mtabiri, wa-, n. forecaster, diviner, prophet/prophetess.
mtafaruku, mi-, n. conflict.
mtaguso, mi-, n. ecumenical council, synod, *Mtaguso Mkuu wa Pili wa Vatican*, Second Ecumenical Council of Vatican.

mtahini, wa-, n. examiner.
mtahiniwa, wa-, n. examinee, examination candidate.
mtaimbo, mi-, n. lever, crowbar.
mtaji, mi-, n. capital, *ukusanyaji wa mitaji*, capital accumulation.
mtakaso, n. cleansing.
mtakatifu, wa-, n. saint, *Mtakatifu Fransisko*, Saint Francis.
mtaliki, wa-, n. divorcer.
mtama, mi-, n. millet.
mtambo, mi-, n. machine with different parts.
mtanashati, wa-, n. smart person, *kijana mtanashati*, smart guy, well dressed and neat person.
mtandao, mi-, n. network, *mtandao wa kimataifa*, international network, also **utandawazi**, globalisation.
mtangawizi, mi-, n. ginger plant.
mtangazaji, wa-, n. broadcaster, advertiser, announcer.
mtangulizi, wa-, n. predecessor.
mtanguo, n. cancellation.
mtani, wa-, n. one in joking relationship.
Mtanzania, wa-, n. Tanzanian.
mtapanyo, n. diffussion.
mtaro, mi-, n. drain(s), sewage system.
mtawa, wa-, n. monk, nun, hermit, friar.
mtawala, wa-, n. ruler, administrator, *watawala wa kikoloni*, colonial rulers.
mtazamaji, wa-, n. spectator, observer.
mtazamo, mi-, n. viewpoint.
mtego, mi-, n. trap.
mteja, wa-, n. customer, client, *wateja wetu*, our clients (customers).
mtemba, mi-, n. smoking pipe.
mtemi, wa-, n. ruler, chief.
mtende, mi-, n. date palm.
mtengenezaji, wa-, n. maker, producer, manufacturer.
mteremko, mi-, n. slope.
mtetezi, wa-, n. defender, advocate, *watetezi wa mazingira*,

environmental advocates.
mteule, wa-, n. appointed figure, selected, nominee.
mti, mi-, n. tree.
mtihani, mi-, n. examination, trial, *mtihani mgumu*, a difficult examination.
mtikiti, mi-, n. water melon plant.
mtima, mi-, n. heart.
mtindi, mi-, n. sour milk, yogurt (colloq.), beer.
mtindo, mi-, n. fashion, style.
mtini, mi-, n. fig tree.
mtiririko, mi-, n. flow.
mto, mi-, n. river 2. pillow.
mtofaa, mi-, n. apple tree.
mtopetope, mi-, n. sugar apple, custard apple.
mtori, mi-, n. green banana soup, famous Chaga dish.
mtoro, wa-, n. runaway, fugitive, dodger.
mtoto, wa-, n. child, *mtoto wa kiume*, son, *mtoto wa kike*, daughter.
mtu, wa-, n. person.
mtuhumiwa, wa-, n. suspect.
mtukutu, wa-, n. naughty person.
mtulivu, wa-, n. calm person.
mtumba, mi-, n. second-hand clothing/material.
mtumbwi, mi-, n. canoe.
mtume, mi-, n. apostle.
mtumishi, wa-, n. servant, *mtumishi wa serikali*, civil servant.
mtundu, wa-, n. mischievous person 2. clever and inventive.
mtungaji, wa-, n. author, composer, originator of a work, writer.
mtungi, mi-, n. water pot.
mtunzi, wa-, n. author, composer, writer, see also **mtungaji**.
mtutu, mi-, n. barrel, muzzle of a gun.
mtwana, wa-, n. slave, serf, *tumekuwa watwana katika nchi yetu*, we have become slaves in our country.
muadhama, wa-, n. eminence.
muarubaini, mi-, n. margosa tree.

muasi-dini, wa-, n. heretic, *amekuwa muasi-dini,* he's become a heretic.

muasisi, wa-, n. founder.

muda, n. period of time.

mudu, ku-, v.t. be able to meet requirements, *kumudu maisha,* to meet life's expenses.

muflisi, adj. bankrupt.

muhimu, adj. important, necessary.

muhindi, ma-, n. maize 2. an Indian.

muhogo, mi-, n. cassava.

muhtasari, mi-, n. summary, compendium.

muhula, mi-, n. term, semester.

muhuri, mi-, n. stamp, seal.

mujibu, n. duty, *kwa mujibu wa,* according to.

muktadha, n. context.

mulika, ku-, v.t. shine on, illuminate, gleam.

mume, wa-, n. husband.

mumunya, ku-, v.t. chew, also **mung'unya, ku-,** v.

mundu, miu-, n. sickle, cutlass.

Mungu, n. God, *Mungu yupo,* God is there! *Mungu wa kweli,* the true God.

murua, adj. something pleasing mentally and physically, honourable.

mustakabali, n. the future, *mustakabali wa taifa letu...,* the future of our nation....

musuli, mi-, n. muscle.

muswada, mi-, n. manuscript, bill of law.

muuaji, wa-, n. killer, terminator, murderer.

muuguzi, wa-, n. nurse.

muujiza, mi-, n. miracle.

muumba, wa-, n. Creator.

muumini, wa-, n. believer, follower, *muumini wa dini ya Kikristo,* a Christian believer.

muungano, n. union, confederation, *Jamhuri ya Muungano ya Tanzania,* United Republic of Tanzania.

muungwana, wa-, n. gentleman/lady, respectful person.

muwa, mi-, n. sugar-cane.

muziki, n. music.

mvi, n. grey hair.

mvinyo   **mwanajeshi**

mvinyo, n. wine.
mviringo, n. curve.
mvua, n. rain.
mvuje, mi-, n. asafoetida tree, gum from asafoetida.
mvuke, n. vapour.
mvulana, wa-, n. boy.
mvule, mi-, n. iroko tree.
mvutano, mi-, n. tension.
mvuvi, wa-, n. fisherman.
mwafaka, mi-, n. consensus, agreement, compromise.
mwaga, ku-, v.t. pour out, spill.
mwagilia, ku-, v.t. irrigate.
mwajiri, waa-, n. employer.
mwajiriwa, waa-, n. employee.
mwaka, mi-, n. year, *mwaka huu*, this year, *mwaka jana*, last year, *mwaka ujao*, next year.
mwale, miale, n. ray, beam, flame.
mwali, wa-, n. teenage girl 2. mi-, n. flame of fire
mwaliko, mi-, n. invitation.
mwalimu, wa-, n. teacher, tutor.

mwamba, mi-, n. rock, pl. miamba.
mwambao, mi-, n. coastal area.
mwamko, mi-, n. awakening.
mwamuzi, wa-, n. referee, arbitrator, mediator, *mwamuzi hakutenda haki,* the referee was unfair.
mwana, wa-, n. son or daughter.
mwanaanga, wa-, n. astronout.
mwanachuo, wa-, n. college/ university student.
mwanadamu, wa-, n. human being.
mwanadiplomasia, wa-, n. diplomat.
mwanafunzi, wa-, n. student.
mwanagenzi, wa-, n. apprentice, learner, trainee.
mwanaharakati, wa-, n. activist.
mwanaisimu, wa-, n. linguist.
mwanajeshi, wa-, n. soldier.

126

mwanamapinduzi   mwendesha-mashtaka

mwanamapinduzi, wa-, n. revolutionary.
mwanamgambo, wa-, n. militia.
mwanamitindo, wa-, n. style model.
mwanamke, wanawake, n. woman.
mwanamume, wa-, n. man, male person.
mwanamuziki, wa-, n. musician.
mwanamwali, wa-, n. maid.
mwanasesere, wa-, n. doll, toy.
mwanasheria, wa-, n. lawyer.
mwanasiasa, wa-, n. politician.
mwanasoka, wa-, n. footballer.
mwanazuoni, wa-, n. scholar.
mwandani, wa-, n. friend (close), confidant.
mwandiko, mi-, n. handwriting, *mwandiko mzuri*, good handwriting.
mwandishi, wa-, n. author, writer, *mwandishi wa habari*, journalist, *mwandishi wa mchezo wa kuigiza*, playwright.
mwanga, mi-, n. light.
mwangwi, n. echo.
mwanya, mi-, n. cleft, gap, loophole.
mwanzi, n. bamboo.
mwanzilishi, wa-, n. founder.
mwanzo, mi-, n. beginning.
mwarabu, wa-, n. arab.
mwasherati, wa-, n. adulterer, fornicator.
mwasho, n. irritation.
mwasi, wa-, n. rebel.
mwasisi, wa-, n. founder.
mwavuli, mi-, n. umbrella.
mwehu, wehu, n. mad person, *je, yule ni mwehu?* Is he mad?
mwelekeo, mi-, n. trend, direction.
mwelewa, welewa, n. knower, those who know.
mwembe, mi-, n. mango tree, *embe*, n. mango.
mwendeshaji, wa-, n. organizer, administrator.
mwendesha-mashtaka,

mwendo

wa-, n. prosecutor.
mwendo, mi-, n. speed, gait, distance.
mwenendo, mi-, n. behaviour, conduct, *mwenendo mwema*, good conduct, demeanour.
mwenge, mi-, n. torch.
mwenyeji, we-, n. native to a place, host, *nchi wenyeji*, hosting country.
Mwenyezi, n. Almighty.
mwenzi, we-, n. companion, partner, *mwenzi katika biashara*, partner in business.
mwerevu, we-, n. clever.
mwezi, mi-, n. moon, month.
mwiba, mi-, n. thorn.
mwigaji, wa-, n. imitator.
mwigizaji, wa-, n. actor/actress, character in a play.
mwigo-bandia, n. counterfeit.
mwiko, mi-, n. taboo, wooden spoon.
mwili, mi-, n. body.
mwimbaji, wa-, n. singer.
mwinamo, n. declivity.
mwindaji, wa-, n. hunter.

mzandiki

mwinjilisti, wa-, n. evangelist.
mwinuko, mi-, n. elevation, up land.
mwisho, mi-, n. end, *mwishoni*, at the end.
Mwislamu, wa-, n. Moslem.
mwitu, msitu, mi-, n. forest.
mwizi, wezi, n. thief, burglar.
mwoga, wa-, n. coward.
mwokozi, wa-, n. redeemer, saviour.
mwongo, wa-, n. liar, *wewe ni mwongo!* you are a liar!
mwongofu, wa-, n. pious person.
mwongozo, mi-, n. guidance.
mwovu, wa-, n. evil person.
mzabibu, mi-, n. grape tree.
mzabuni, wa-, n. bidder, tenderer.
mzaha, mi-, n. joke, *fanya mzaha*, make fun.
mzamiaji, wa-, n. stowaway 2. n. diver.
mzandiki, wa-, n.

hypocrite, liar.
mzawa, wa-, n. native.
mzazi, wa-, n. parent.
mzee, wa-, n. old man.
mzeituni, mi-, n. olive tree.
mzigo, mi-, n. load, *beba mzigo*.
mzimu, mi-, n. dead person's spirit that wonders about.
mzinga, mi-, canon.
mzingo, mi-, n. circumference, *mzingo wa dunia*, earth circumference.
mzinifu, wa-, n. adulterer.
mzinzi, wa-, n. promiscuous person.
mzio, n. allergy.
mziwanda, wa-, n. last born child.
mzizi, mi-, n. root.
mzoga, mi-, n. corpse.
mzugo, mi-, n. hypnotism.
mzuka, mi-, n. harmful spirit.
mzungu, wa-, n. European, white person.
mzunguko, mi-, n. circulation, going round.
mzungusho, mi-, n. circulation.
mzushi, wa-, n. one who invents stories to cause mischief.
mzuzu, mi-, n. plantain.

N

na, conj. and, with, *mimi na mama*, mother and I (literally).

naam, interj. yes, indeed.

nabii, ma-, n. prophet, prophetess, *nabii wa uongo*, false prophet.

nadharia, n. theory.

nadhifisha, ku-, v.t. make neat, tiden up.

nadhifu, adj. clean, neat, smart.

nadhiri, n. vow, *weka nadhiri za milele*, make perpetual vows.

nadi, ku-, v.t. sell at auction 2. v. wake up people for morning prayers (for Moslems)

nadra, adv. seldom, rarely.

nafaka, n. corn, grain, cereal.

nafasi, n. space, occasion, *pata nafasi*, have opportunity.

nafsi, n. self, *mimi binafsi*, I myself, person, ego.

nafuu, n. relief, *pata nafuu*, feel better (sick), cheaper, *bei nafuu*, better price.

nahau, n. idiomatic expression.

nahodha, ma-, n. captain, *nahodha wa timu yetu*, our team captain.

naibu, ma-, n. deputy, *naibu waziri*, deputy minister, assistant.

nailoni, n. nylon, *mifuko ya nailoni*, plastic bags.

najisi, n. dirt, impurity 2. **ku-,** v.i. soil, abuse, sexually, contaminate.

nakala, n. copy.

nakili, ku-, v.t. copy, make a copy.

nakisi, n. deficit 2. reduce.

nakshi, ku-, v.t. decorate, curve.

namba, n. number.

nambari, n. number.

nami, (na **mimi**), pers. pron. with me, and I.

namna, n. sort, kind, how, type, *fanya namna hii*, do it this way.

nana, n. madam.

nanasi, n. pineapple.
nane, adj. eight (8).
nanga, n. anchor.
nani? interrog. pron. who? *nani wewe?* who are you?
nasa, ku-, v.i. catch in a trap, cf. *kamata*.
nasaba, n. relationship, lineage.
nasaha, n. sound counselling, *toa nasaha kwa vijana*, give counselling to youth.
nasi, pers. pron. with us, and us, *wanaishi nasi*, they live with us.
nasibu, adv. chance, luck.
nasua, ku-, v.t. set free from a trap.
nata, ku-, v.i. be sticky, stick.
nati, n. nut.
nauli, n. fare, *toa, lipa nauli*, pay the fare.
nawa, ku-, v.t. wash hands and face.
nawe, pers. pron. with you (*na wewe*).
nawiri, ku-, v.i. prosper, be successful, become healthy.
naye, pers. pron. with him or her.

nazi, n. coconut.
ncha, n. point, tip.
nchi, n. land, *nchi yetu*, our country.
ndala, ndara, n. sandals, slippers, *tumia ndala zangu*, use my slippers.
ndama, n. calf.
ndani, adv. inside, *ndani ya nyumba*, inside the house.
ndarire, n. useless talk.
ndege, n. bird 2. aircraft, aeroplane.
nderemo, n. celebration.
ndevu, pl. (sing. **udevu**) beard.
ndezi, n. kind of rat usually big in size.
ndilo, pron. *hilo*, that's it (ni hilo).
ndimi, n. (pl. of **ulimi**) tongue 2. it's me (**ni mimi**).
ndimu, n. lime.
ndipo, pron. that's when, *ndipo akaniambia*, that's when he told me, that's where, *ni hapo*.
ndiyo, interj. acceptance, agree with, *ni hiyo*, yes, it is that (thing).
ndizi, n. banana.

ndoa

ndoa, n. marriage; *funga ndoa,* solemnise marriage, *fungisha ndoa,* officiate marriage.
ndoana, n. hook for catching fish.
ndondi, n. boxing; *pigana ndondi,* fight in a boxing match.
ndonga, n. thick stick, sharp kick, short club.
ndoo, n. bucket.
ndorobo, n. tsetse-fly.
ndoto, n. dream, *ndoto yangu,* my dream.
ndovu, n. elephant.
ndui, n. smallpox.
ndumba, n. magic.
ndumilakuwili, n. hypocrite.
ndururu, adj. small.
neema, n. grace, affluence, bounty.
neemeka, ku-, v.i. be in affluence, be rich.
neemesha, ku-, v.t. make affluent.
nembo, n. symbol, sign, logo, *nembo ya kampuni,* company's logo.
nena, ku-, v.i. speak, see **sema,** say.

ng'ang'ana

nenda, v.i. imper. go, *nendeni,* go (pl.).
nene, adj. fat (of people).
nenepa, ku-, v.i. grow fat.
nenepesha, ku-, v.t. cause to be fat.
nengua, ku-, v.i. sway one's hips.
neno, ma-, n. word.
neno-hitimisha, n. epilogue.
nepa, ku-, v.i. bend due to weight.
nepi, n. nappy.
netiboli, n. netball.
neva, n. nerve.
ng'aa, ng'ara, ku-, v.i. shine, glitter, *si vyote ving'aravyo ni dhahabu,* not all that glitters is gold.
ng'aka, ku-, v.i. retort, shout at.
ng'ambo, n. the other side of the river or road, overseas, *amekwenda ng'ambo,* he has gone overseas/abroad.
ng'amua, ku-, v.t. find out, understand, discern, detect.
ng'ang'ana, ng'ang'ania, ku-, v. refuse to let go,

ng'ara   ngome-mji

maintain one's point, stick to.
ng'ara, ku-, v.i. shine, glitter, see also **ng'aa**.
ng'arisha, ku-, v.t. polish, shine.
ng'ata, ku-, v.t. bite.
ng'atuka, ku-, v.i. to step down from power, *ameng'atuka kwa hiari yake mwenyewe*, he has stepped down willingly, retire.
ng'o, adv. never, *sikupi ng'o!* I will never give you!.
ng'oa, ku-, v.t. uproot, dig up.
ng'oka, v.t. be uprooted.
ng'ombe, n. cow, bull, cattle.
ng'onda, n. split dried fish.
ng'ong'o, n. small roundish type of mangoes with fibres inside.
ngadu, n. crab.
ngalawa, n. canoe.
ngambi, n. confederation.
ngamia, n. camel.
ngano, n. wheat 2. a story, a tale, fable.

ngao, n. shield, *ngao yako i wapi?* where is your shield?
ngapi? interrog. how many? *watu wangapi?* how many people? *viti vingapi?* how many chairs?
ngariba, n. circumciser.
ngawira, n. loot, booty.
ngazi, n. ladder, *achia ngazi*, step down, retire.
nge, n. scorpion.
ngedere, n. monkey.
ngeli, n. noun class.
ngeu, n. a cut on the head by a stick when fighting.
ngiri, n. wild pig 2. swollen scrotum, hernia.
ngisi, n. cuttlefish.
ngogo, n. catfish.
ngoja, ku-, v.t. wait, *ngoja kidogo*, wait a bit/moment.
ngojea, ku-, v.t. wait for somebody or something, *unamngojea nani?* whom are you waiting for?
ngoma, n. drum 2. dance, *kucheza ngoma*, to dance.
ngome, n. fortress, castle.
ngome-mji, mi-, n. citadel.

ngonjera, n. poem recited in turn by several characters.
ngono, n. sexual intercourse, *ni mgonjwa wa ngono*, he is a sex maniac.
ngozi, n. skin, leather.
nguchiro, n. mongoose.
ngumi, n. fist, *piga ngumi*, hit somebody with a fist.
nguo, n. cloth, clothes, *vaa nguo*, put on clothes.
nguru, n. kingfish.
nguruma, ku-, v.i. roar.
ngurumo, n. roar, thunder.
nguruwe, n. pig, *nguruwe pori*, wild pigs.
nguva, n. mermaid, manatee.
nguvu, n. strength, force, *kwa nguvu*, by force.
nguvukazi, n. labour force.
nguzo, n. pillar, post.
ngwe, n. farming plot alloted for a particular time of labour.
ngwena, n. crocodile.
ni, v.i. am, is, are.
nia, n. intention, purpose, aim.

niaba, n. *kwa niaba ya*, on behalf of.
nidhamu, n. discipline.
nikotini, n. nicotine.
nimonia, n. pneumonia.
ning'inia, ku-, v.i. hang on something.
ning'iniza, ku-, v.t. hang/suspend sth.
nini? interrog. pron. what? *kwa nini?* why?
ninyi, pers. pron. you (pl.).
nipo, v. I am present, also kuwepo, to be.
niru, n. oxygen residue used to paint walls before the proper colour, sludge lime.
nishai, n. state of drunkenness.
nishani, n. medal, prize.
nishati, n. energy.
nitrojeni, n. nitrogen.
njaa, n. hunger, famine, *ona, sikia njaa*, feel hungry.
njama, n. plot to do something evil, *fanya njama*, plot to do something evil.
njano, n. yellow.
nje, adv. outside, *nje ya*

nyumba, outside the house, *nenda nje,* go outside.

njegere, n. pea.

njemba, ma-, n. giant of man.

njia, n. way, *njiani*, on the way.

njiti, n. tooth pick, premature infant, *ulizaliwa njiti*, you were born premature.

njiwa, n. dove.

njoo, n. come.

njozi, n. dream, vision, *msichana wa njozi yangu*, my dream girl.

njuga, n. little bells worn on the legs by dancers.

njugu, n. peanuts, groundnuts.

nne, adj. four (4).

noa, ku-, v.t. sharpen, *noa kisu*, sharpen a knife 2. to miss one's target, *nimenoa*, I've missed it.

noeli, n. christmas.

noga, ku-, v.i. be very tasty, be good.

nokoa, ma-, n. assistant farm supervisor/guard.

nomino, n. noun.

nona, ku-, v.i. be fat (animal, meat).

nondo, n. a bar of iron used for building 2. moth.

nong'oneza, ku-, v.i. address somebody in a whisper.

nongo'ona, ku-, v.i. whisper.

nono, adj. fat (animal, meat).

noti, n. bank note.

notisi, n. notice, *toa notisi ya miezi mitatu*, give a three months notice.

Novemba, n. November.

nta, n. wax.

nufaika, ku-, v.i. profit from, gain, *tumenufaika vya kutosha kwenye semina hii*, we have gained a lot in this seminar.

nufaisha, ku-, v.t. profit sb.

nuia, ku-, v.i. intend, decide to.

nuka, ku-, v.i. stink, smell bad.

nukia, ku-, v.i. have a good smell.

nuksi, n. bad luck, bad omen.

nukta

nukta, n. full stop, period, point, *mpaka nukta hii,* up to this point.
nuna, ku-, v.i. look glumy refuse to speak, be sullen.
nundu, ma-, n. a swelling, bat.
nundu, n. hump.
nung'unika, ku-, v.t. complain, grumble.
nung'unikia, ku-, v.t. complain to somebody about something.
nung'uniko, ma-, n. grievances.
nunia, ku-, v.t. refuse to speak to somebody.
nunua, ku-, v.t. buy.
nunulia, ku-, v.t. buy something for somebody.
nuru, n. light.
nururisha, ku-, v.t. radiate, lighten.
nusa, ku-, v.t. smell.
nusra, adv. almost, nearly.
nusu, n. half, *nusu saa,* half an hour.
nusukaputi, n. chloroform.
nusukipenyo, nusuvipenyo, n. radius, radii.

nyani

nusura, prep. almost, nearly; *nusura afe,* he almost died.
nusurika, ku-, v.i. escape unhurt.
nusuru, ku-, v.t. save from danger, defend.
nya, ku-, v.i. defecate.
nyafua, ku-, v.t. chop off, tear off.
nyakanga, n. main instructor during initiation.
nyakati, n. time (sing. **wakati**).
nyakua, ku-, v.t. snatch off.
nyama, n. meat.
nyamafu, n. dead body of animal, unclean meat from a carcass, tainted meat.
nyamaza, ku-, v.i. be silent, also **nyamaa**.
nyambizi, ma-, n. submarine.
nyambulisha, ku-, v.t. derive words in sentences.
nyang'anya, ku-, v.t. rob, take by force, confiscate (lawfully).
nyani, n. ape, monkey.

136

nyanya

nyanya, n. tomato 2. n. grandmother, *nyanya yangu ni mzee sana*, my grandmother is very old.
nyanyasa, ku-, v.t. to oppress, treat badly.
nyanyua, ku-, v.t. lift something.
nyara, n. booty, *teka nyara*, hijack.
nyaraka, n. documents (sing. **waraka**)
nyasi, n. tall grass, reed.
nyata, ku-, v.i. sneak, *nyatia*, steal upon.
nyati, n. buffalo.
nyauka, ku-, v.i. dry up.
nyayo, n. foot prints.
nyea, ku-, v.i. fall on somebody (rain), defecate on.
nyege, n. sexual feelings.
nyemelea, ku-, v.t. creep upon.
nyenje, n. cricket.
nyenyekea, ku-, v.t. be humble, to be obedient.
nyenyekevu, adj. humble.
nyenyere, n. very tiny black ant.
nyenzo, n. lever, tools.
nyesha, ku-, v.i. rain, *mvua imenyesha*, it has rained.

nyonya

nyeti, adj. crucial, sensitive.
nyigu, n. wasp, hornet.
nyika, n. steppe.
nyima, ku-, v.t. refuse to give something to somebody, to deny somebody something.
nyingi, adj. many, a lot of, *sukari nyingi*, a lot of, too much of.
nyinyi, pers. pron. you, *nyinyi wawili*, you two.
nyoa, ku-, v.t. shave, cut hair off
nyofoa, ku-, v.t. tear off.
nyofu, adj. honest, sincere, candid, righteous, *mtu mnyofu*, a righteous person.
nyoka, n. snake, serpant.
nyong'onyea, ku-, v.i. to lose energy, to weaken, feel weak, be depressed, enervate.—
nyonga, ku-, v.t. hang by the neck.
nyonge, adj. weak, powerless, feeble.
nyongeza, n. addition.
nyongo, n. bile.
nyonya, ku-, v.t. suck mother's breast.

nyonyesha   nzige

nyonyesha, ku-, v.t. suckle, to breast feed.
nyonyo, ma-, n. nipple, teat.
nyooka, ku-, v.i. be straight.
nyoosha, ku-, v.t. straighten.
nyota, n. star, *wachezaji nyota*, star players.
nyoyo, n. hearts (sing. **moyo**).
nyuka, ku-, v.t. beat (somebody) thoroughly.
nyuki, n. bee, *fuata nyuki ule asali*, follow bees so as to eat honey (prov.).
nyuma, adv. behind, *nyuma yangu*, behind me, *nyuma ya nyumba*, behind the house.
nyumba, n. house(s), *nyumba ya kisasa*, modern house.
nyumbuliwa, ku-, v.i. be extended.
nyundo, n. hammer.

nyungunyungu, n. kind of worm living in mud.
nyunyiza, ku-, v.t. sprinkle, *nyunyizia*, sprinkle on, to somebody or something.
nyuso, n. faces (sing. **uso**, face).
nyuzi, n. threads (sing. **uzi**, thread).
nyuzijoto, n. temperature measurement, degree.
nywa, ku-, v.t. drink, *kunywa maji mengi*, drink a lot of water.
nywea, ku-, v.i. shrink, be weak 2. drink from, *nywea kikombe hiki*, drink from this cup.
nywele, n. hair (sing. **unywele**).
nywesha, ku-, v.t. give water to drink, help a child or animal to drink.
nzi, n. fly, domestic fly.
nzige, n. locust.

O

oa, ku-, v.t. marry (of man), *John ameoa,* John has got married.
oana, ku-, v.t. marry one another, be compatible.
oanisha, ku-, v.t. make compatible.
oda, n. order 2. **ku-,** v.t. to order.
ofisa, ma-, n. officer.
ofisi, n. office.
oga, ku-, v.i. take a bath.
ogelea, ku-, v.i. swim.
ogesha, ku-, v.t. bathe somebody.
ogofya, ku-, v.t. frighten, confound.
ogopa, ku-, v.t. be afraid of, fear.
ogopesha, ku-, v.t. frighten.
oka, ku-, v.t. bake, *oka mkate,* bake bread.
okoa, ku-, v.t. save, rescue.
okota, ku-, v.t. pick up.
oksijeni, n. oxygen.
Oktoba, n. October.
ole, n. woe, *ole wako,* woe upon you.
olewa, ku-, v.i. be married (of woman), *Asha ameolewa,* Asha has been married.
olimpiki, n. olympic.
omba, ku-, v.t. pray for, ask for, apply for.
ombaomba, n. beggar.
ombea, ku-, v.t. pray for, intercede for.
ombi, ma-, n. petition, request.
omboleza, ku-, v.t. condole, weep, lament, mourn.
ombolezo, ma-, n. lamentation, mourning.
ona, ku-, v.t. see, consider.
onana, ku-, v.t. see each other, meet, *tutaonana baadaye,* we shall meet later.
ondoa, ku-, v.t. remove also **ondosha**.
ondoka, ku-, v.i. leave, go away.
ondolea, ku-, v.t. forgive, absolve,

ondosha, ku-, v.t. eliminate, see **ondoa**.

onea, ku-, v.t. oppress, bully.

onekana, ku-, v.i. be visible, be seen.

onelea, ku-, v.i. be of the opinion, *mimi naonelea kwamba*, I'm of the opinion that.

onesha, ku-, v.t. to show, *nioneshe njia*, show me the way, see **onyesha**.

onevu, adj. cruel, oppressive.

ongea, ku-, v.t. speak, talk, *ongea kwa sauti*, talk loudly.

ongeza, ku-, v.t. increase, add to.

ongezeko, n. addition.

ongezi, ma-, n. conversation.

ongopa, ku-, v.t. tell a lie.

ongoza, ku-, v.t. lead, *ongoza maandamano*, lead procession.

ongozana, ku-, v.i. walk along together, follow one another.

onja, ku-, v.t. taste.

onjesha, ku-, v.t. give somebody something to taste.

onya, ku-, v.t. warn, *nakuonya*, I warn you.

onyesha, ku-, v.t. show, see **onesha**.

onyesho, ma-, n. exhibition.

onyo, ma-, n. warning, *onya*, warn, *onyo kali*, stern, strong, warning.

operesheni, n. operation.

opereta, ma-, n. operator.

opoa, ku-, v.t. to take something out of a liquid container, remove a cooking pot from fire.

orodha, n. list, catalogue.

orodhesha, ku-, v.t. give a list of.

osha, ku-, v.t. wash.

ota, ku-, v.i. grow, germinate 2. dream, *ota ndoto mbaya*, have a bad dream.

ote, adj. all, *watu wote*, all people, *vitu vyote*, all things.

otea, ku-, v.i. (in football) be off-side.

otesha, ku-, v.t. to plant, *otesha miti*, plant trees.

ovataimu, n. overtime, *malipo ya ovataimu*, payment for overtime.

ovu

ovu, ma-, n. evil deeds, bad things.
ovyo, adj. carelessly.
oyee! interj. hurrah!

oza

oza, ku-, v.i. rɔt, go bad, *embe hili limeoza*, this mango is rotten.

P

pa, ku-, v.t. give, *amekupa nini?* what has he given you?

paa, ku-, v.i. ascend 2. n. roof 3. n. gazelle 4. v.t. remove fish scales.

paaza, v.t. raise, *kipaaza sauti*, loud speaker.

pacha, ma-, n. twin.

pachika, ku-, v.t. place something between other things.

padri, ma-, n. priest.

pafu, ma-, n. lung.

pagaa, ku-, v.t. possess (of spirits) somebody, *amepagawa*, he is possessed (by evil spirits).

pahali, n. place.

paja, ma-, n. thigh.

pajama, ma-, n. pyjamas.

paji, ma-, n. forehead, *paji la uso*, forehead.

paka, n. cat 2. v.t. paint, *paka nyumba rangi*, paint a house.

pakaa, same as paka.

pakana, ku-, v.t. lie next to, have common border with.

pakata, ku-, v.t. hold fondly on the laps.

pakia, ku-, v.t. load on, *pakia mizigo/watu*, take luggage/people on the car.

pakiti, n. packet, *pakiti ya maziwa*, milk packet.

pakua, ku-, v.t. unload, *pakua mizigo*, unload luggage.

pale, adv. there, *hapa na pale*, here and there.

palia, palilia, ku-, v.t. weed.

palilia, ku-, v.t. weed.

pamba, n. cotton 2. v.t. adorn, decorate.

pambaja, ku-, v.t. embrace.

pambamoto, ku-, v.i. intensify.

pambana, ku-, v.t. confront, engage in battle, *pambana na adui*, engage the enemy in battle.

pambana   **paparika**

pambanua, ku-, v.t. analyse, explain, discern.
pambazuka, ku-, v.i. dawn, *kumepambazuka*, it is dawn.
pambazuko, ma-, n. dawn.
pambo, ma-, n. decoration, ornament.
pamoja, adv. together, *pamoja na*, together with.
pampu, n. pamp.
pana, adj. wide, *panapo na*, where there is. *panapo nia pana njia*, where there is will there is a way.
pancha, n. puncture.
panchi, ku-, v.t. punch.
panda, ku-, v.t. go up 2. v.t. plant.
pandashuka, v.t. fluctuate.
pande, ma-, n. a big piece, *pande la mtu*, a giant.
pandikizi, ma-, n. giant.
pandisha, ku-, v.t. raise, bring something upwards, elevate, conduct natural insermination (to animals), *pandisha mashetani*, be possessed by evil spirits.
paneli, n. panel.
panga, ku-, v. arrange 2. rent a room 3. big knife (pl. **mapanga**).
pangaboi, ma-, n. propeller, ceiling fan.
pangisha, ku-, v.t. rent rooms to people.
pango, ma-, n. cave, *Mapango ya Amboni*, the Amboni Caves, den, *pango la wezi*, thieves' den.
pangua, ku-, v.t. disarrange.
pangusa, ku-, v.t. wipe, *pangusa jasho*, wipe sweat, *pangusa meza*, wipe the table.
pania, ku-, v.i. aim at doing sth strongly.
panua, ku-, v.t. widen.
panya, n. rat, mouse.
panzi, n. grass-hopper.
papa, n. shark 2. n. Pope, *Baba Mtakatifu*, the Holy Father.
papai, ma-, n. pawpaw.
papara, n. haste, speed, *usifanye papara*, do not make haste.
paparika, ku-, v.i. plutter.

papasa, ku-, v.t. touch, stroke, grope.
papasi, ma-, n. tick.
papi, n. long post for roofing.
papo hapo, on the spot.
parachichi, ma-, n. avocado.
paradiso, n. paradise.
paraganya, ku-, v.t. mix up.
paramia, ku-, v.t. mount 2. do something above one's ability.
paramia, ku-, v.t. mount on, take on sth without much care, climb on.
parandesi, n. bracket.
parapanda, n. trumpet, last trump.
paredi, n. parade.
parokia, ma-, n. parish, *ukumbi wa parokia*, parish hall.
paroko, ma-, n. parish priest, *paroko msaidizi*, assistant parish priest.
parua, parura, ku-, v.t. scratch.
paruza, ku-, v.t. rub, graze.
Pasaka, n. Easter, Paschal.
pasha, ku-, v. inform, *pasha habari*, give information 2. *pasha moto*, warm up, *pasha chai moto*, warm up tea.
pasi, n. iron for pressing clothes 2. v.t. ku-, pass, *pasi mtihani*, pass one's exams.
pasipo, prep. without.
pasipoti, n. passport.
pasisha, ku-, v.t. authorise, cause to pass.
pasua, ku-, v.t. break, tear up.
pasuka, ku-, v.i. be split.
paswa, ku-, v.i. see pasa, v.i. oblige, *yanipasa*, I must, *ninapaswa, inanipasa*, I am obliged to.
pata, ku-, v.t. get, *pata habari*, be informed.
patana, ku-, v.i. agree together, be reconciled.
patanisha, ku-, v.t. reconcile, arbitrate, harmonise.
patano, ma-, n. agreement.
patashika, n. commotion.
patasi, n. chisel.
patia, ku-, v.t. give something to somebody,

patikana

amenipatia chumba, he has given me a room, he has found a room for me, do something in the right way.

patikana, ku-, v.i. be obtainable or available.

pato, ma-, n. income, earnings.

paua, ku-, v.t. roof a house.

pauka, ku-, v.i. fade, loose the original colour.

paukwa! interj. expressing beginning of a tale/story.

pauni, n. pound.

payuka, ku-, v.i. talk unguardedly, shout.

paza, ku-, v.t. raise.

pazia, n. curtain, *macho hayana pazia*; eyes see whatever is there, even shameful sights.

peasi, ma-, n. pear fruit.

pedeli, n. pedal.

pekecha, ku-, v.t. bore, drill, stir.

pekee, adj. alone, solitary.

pekua, ku-, v.t. search, leave no stone unturned.

pekupeku, adv. barefooted.

peleka, ku-, v.t. send, convey.

pendelea

pelekea, ku-, v.t. send something to somebody, *alinipelekea kifurushi*, he sent the parcel for me.

peleleza, ku-, v.t. investigate, spy upon.

pembe, n. corner, horn, *pembeni*, at the corner, on the side.

pembejeo, n. tools, implements.

pembekali, n. acute angle.

pembemraba, n. right angle.

pembetatu mraba, n. right angled triangle.

pembetatu pacha, n. congruent angle.

pembetatu sawa, n. equilateral triangle.

pembetatu, n. triangle.

penda, ku-, v.t. love, like, *nakupenda*, I love you, *napenda chai*, I like tea.

pendeka, ku-, v.i. be loved, be worth loving.

pendekeza, ku-, v.t. recommend.

pendekezo, ma-, n. proposal, suggestion.

pendelea, ku-, v.t. treat

pendeza   piga

partially, show favour.
pendeza, ku-, v.t. please somebody, be pleasant.
pendo, ma-, n. love.
penga, ku-, v.t. blow one's nose.
pengine, adv. may be, perhaps, probably, also see **labda**.
pengo, ma-, n. gap, defect, *kuna pengo*, there is something missing.
peni, n. pen.
peninsula, n. peninsula.
penseli, n. pencil.
pentekoste, n. pentecost.
penya, ku-, v.i. penetrate, squeeze something through.
penyeza, ku-, v.t. sneak in, enter unnoticed or cleverly.
penzi, ma-, n. love between lovers, *fanya mapenzi*, make love, have sex.
pepea, ku-, v.i. fly in the air like a flag, *bendera inapepea*, the flag is flying in the air.
peperusha, ku-, v.t. blow away.
pepesa, ku-, v.t. blink the eyes.

pepesuka, ku-, v.i. swing back and forth like a drunkard.
pepeta, ku-, v.t. winnow.
pepo, n. winds, 2. evil spirits, ghosts, *ana pepo*, he is possessed.
pepopunda, n. tetanus.
pera, ma-, n. guava, pear.
perege, n. tilapia fish.
peremende, n. sweet, mint.
pesa, n. money, cash.
pete, n. ring, *pete na kidole*, ring and finger, symbol of close friendship.
pevu, adj. mature, ripe.
pevua, ku-, v.t. cause to know the facts of life, cause to mature, rippen.
pevuka, ku-, v.i. come of age, become mature.
pewa, ku-, v.t. be given, *amepewa vitu*, he has been given things.
pezi, ma-, n. fish fin.
pia, adv. also, *mimi pia*, I too.
picha, n. picture, *piga picha*, take a photograph.
piga, ku-, v.t. strike, beat,

pigana — pishana

piga mbio, run.
pigana, ku-, v.t. fight one another.
pigania, ku-, v.i. fight for, struggle for something.
piganisha, ku-, v.t. cause two to fight one another.
pigano, ma-, n. battle, fight.
pigo, ma-, n. beat, *mapigo ya moyo*, heart beats.
pika, ku-, v.t. cook.
pikipiki, n. motorbike.
piku, ku-, v.t. outdo somebody, win a game of cards.
pili, adv. secondly.
pilipili, n. pepper.
pima, ku-, v.t. measure, weigh.
pimajoto, n. thermometer.
pimia, ku-, v.t. weigh something for somebody, *ametupimia kilo kumi*, he has weighed 10 kg for us.
pinda, ku-, v.t. bend, twist something, *njia imepinda*, the road is bent, seam, *pinda nguo*, have your clothes seamed.
pindi, adv. meanwhile, *pindi akija*, as soon as he comes.
pindika, ku-, v.i. be bent, be twisted, be seamed.
pindo, ma-, n. hem.
pindua, ku-, v.t. turn over, overthrow.
pinduka, ku-, v.i. over turn, *gari limepinduka*, the car has overturned.
pindukia, ku-, v.i. turn toward, *pindukia huku*, turn towards here, *ni mwizi kupindukia*, he is an incorrigible thief with a long record.
pinga, ku-, v.t. oppose, *pingana*, oppose each other, disagree.
pingamizi, vi-, n. obstacle, *ondoa vipingamizi*, remove (take away) obstacles.
pingili, n. knot, plant joints.
pingu, n. handcuff, fetter.
pini, n. pin.
pinki, n. pink.
pipa, n. barrel, cask.
piramidi, n. pyramid.
pisha, ku-, v.t. let pass, *nipishe*, let me pass.
pishana, ku-, v.i. cross

pita   **ponyoka**

each other 2. differ in age, height, opinion, weight, etc.
pita, ku-, v.i. pass, surpass.
pitia, ku-, v.i. pass by 2. review a book.
pitika, ku-, v.i. be passable.
pitiliza, ku-, v.i. surpass.
pitisha, ku-, v.t. allow to pass, *pitisha sheria*, promulgate a law.
pitiwa, ku-, v.i. to fail to notice, forget.
plastiki, n. plastic.
po, rel. pron. when, *alipokuja*, when he came.
poa, ku-, v.i. cool down.
pochi, n. purse, handbag.
poda, n. powder, *poda ya watoto*, baby powder.
pofua, ku-, v.t. cause blindness.
pofuka, ku-, v.i. become blind.
pofusha, ku-, v.t. see **pofua**.
pogoa, ku-, v.t. prune.
pointi, n. point, *amepata pointi tano*, he has got five points.

pokea, ku-, v.t. receive, accept, *tumepokea oda yako*, we have received your order.
pokezana, ku-, v.t. take turns.
pokonya, ku-, v.t. rob, snatch off, grab from.
pole! adv. I am sorry! 2. adj. gentle, quiet, *mtu mpole*, a quiet person.
polepole, adv. slowly.
polisi, ma-, n. police, *jeshi la polisi*, police force.
pombe, n. liquor, beer, etc.
pona, ku-, v.i. recover, *amepona*, he has recovered.
ponda, ku-, v.t. crush, pound, *pondaponda*, crush to pieces.
pondeka, ku-, v.i. be crushed.
pongeza, ku-, v.t. congratulate, *tunakupongeza*, we congratulate you.
pongezi, ma-, n. congratulation.
poni, n. pawn.
ponya, ku-, v.t. cure.
ponyoka, ku-, v.i. slip away, escape.

ponza

ponza, ku-, v.t. cause trouble for someone.
pooza, ku-, v.i. paralyse.
popo, n. bat.
popote, adv. everywhere, anywhere.
pora, ku-, v.t. rob, snatch, loot, *majeshi ya kigeni yalipora utajiri wetu,* foreign troops looted our wealth.
pori, n. jungle, bush, *porini,* in the bush.
porojo, n. idle talk, chitchat.
poromoa, ku-, v.t. see **bomoa,** demolish.
poromoka, ku-, v.i. crumble down, fall down.
poromoko, ma-, n. fall, *maporomoko ya maji,* waterfall.
posa, ku-, v.t. ask in marriage, betrothe.
posho, n. ration.
posta, n. post office.
potea, ku-, v.i. get lost, go astray.
poteza, ku-, v.t. lose, *poteza fahamu,* lose one's senses, *poteza damu,* haemorrhage.

pumbaza

potoa, ku-, v.t. ruin, lead astray.
potoka, ku-, v.i. go astray, err.
potosha, ku-, v.t. lead astray, mislead, *habari za kupotosha,* misleading story, demoralize.
povu, ma-, n. foam, lather.
presha, n. pressure.
programu, n. programme.
propaganda, n. propaganda.
protini, n. protein.
protokali, n. protocol.
pua, n. nose.
puliza, ku-, v.t. blow on a fire to make it burn, blow to cool something.
pulizia, ku-, v.t. blow on, into, at, blow on something hot to cool it, inflate.
pulizo, ma-, n. balloon.
pumba, ma-, n. chaff.
pumbaa, ku-, v.i. be dumbfounded, feel lost, confused.
pumbavu, adj. foolish, stupid.
pumbaza, ku-, v.t.

confuse, hypnotise.
pumbu, ma-, n. testicles.
pumua, ku-, v.i. breathe.
pumzi, n. breath, *pumzi ndefu*, deep breath.
pumzika, ku-, v.i. rest, stop working.
pumziko, ma-, n. resting, leave, break, be off work.
pumzisha, ku-, v.t. cause to rest, put to rest.
punda, n. donkey, ass, *pundamilia*, zebra.
punde, n. period, *punde si punde*, in a little while.
punga, ku-, v.t. wave, *punga upepo*, go for a walk.
pungia, ku-, v.t. wave at somebody, *alitupungia mkono*, he waved at us.
pungua, ku-, v.i. become less, diminish, go down in quantity/quality.
punguani, n. simpleton.
pungufu, adj. deficient, less.
punguka, ku-, v.i. dwindle, see also **pungua**.
punguza, ku-, v.t. reduce, cut down, condense.
punja, ku-, v.t. cheat in a transaction, dupe.
punje, n. grain, *punje ya mchele*, rice grain.
punjika, ku-, v.i. lose in an exchange of things.
punyeto, n. masturbation.
pupa, n. excessive eagerness, *fanya kwa pupa*, do something rashly.
puto, ma-, n. balloon.
pwa, ku-, v.i. dry up, *maji kupwa*, low tide.
pwani, n. coast.
pwaya, ku-, v.i. be loose, hang loosely.
pweke, adj. lonely.
pweza, n. cuttle fish.
pwita, ku-, v.i. pulse.
pya, adj. new, *kitu kipya*, a new thing.

R

raba, n. rubber shoes.
Rabi, n. God, Lord.
rabsha, n. trouble, *fanya rabsha*, cause trouble.
rada, n. radar.
radhi, n. pardon, *kunradhi*, pardon me.
radi, n. clap of thunder, lightining.
rafiki, ma-, n. friend, *rafiki wa kike*, girl friend.
rafu, adj. rough 2. shelf 3. foul.
raghba, n. interest.
raha, n. comfort, bliss, *raha mustarehe*, live in luxury, *ona raha*, feel comfortable.
rahani, n. store, pawn, security.
rahisi, adj. easy, *hili ni swali rahisi*, this is an easy question, cheap.
rahisisha, ku-, v.t. simplify.
rai, n. opinion, advice, point of view.
raia, n. citizen, civilian, *haki za kiraia*, civil rights.
rais, n. president, *Rais wa Kenya*, Kenyan president.
rajamu, n. trade-mark.
rakamu, n. figure, number.
raketi, n. racket.
Ramadhani, n. Ramadan, Moslem's holy month.
ramani, n. map.
rambirambi, n. condolences.
ramli, n. divination, *piga ramli*, consult the diviner.
ramsa, n. celebration.
ranchi, n. ranch.
randa, n. plane, *randa mbao*, plane timber.
randaranda, ku-, v.i. to walk about aimlessly, walk aimlessly.
rangi, n. colour.
rarua, ku-, v.t. tear up, *rarua shati*, tear a shirt.
raruka, ku-, v.i. be torn up.
rasharasha, n. light rain.

rashia, v.t. sprinkle.
rasi, n. promontory, cape.
rasilimali, n. natural resources, capital.
rasmi, adj. official.
rasta, n. rasta.
rasuli, n. God's messenger, prophet.
ratiba, n. time-table, arrangement, schedule.
ratibu, ku-, v.t. coordinate, arrange.
ratili, n. pound.
raundi, n. round.
redio, n. radio.
rediokaseti, n. radio cassette.
ree, n. ace.
refa, n. referee.
refu, adj. tall, long, deep.
refuka, ku-, v.i. grow tall, *amerefuka sana*, he has grown very tall.
refusha, ku-, v.t. lengthen, elongate.
rehani, n. pawn, security.
rehema, n. mercy, grace.
rejareja, adv. retail sale.
rejea, ku-, v.i. return, come back, go back.
rejesha, ku-, v.t. give back.
rejesta, n. register.
rekebisha, ku-, v.t. correct, rectify.
rekodi, n. records 2. v.t. record something.
rekodiplea, n. record player.
reli, n. railway.
remba, ku-, v.t. decorate.
rembo, ma-, n. decoration, see **urembo**.
rembua, ku-, v.t. to make eye movements to seduce (said of women).
rembulia, ku-, v.t. see **rembua**.
riadha, n. athletics game.
riba, n. usury, interest, *kopesha kwa riba,* lend at interest.
riboni, n. ribbon.
ridhaa, n. willingness, agreement, consent.
ridhia, ku-, v.i. approve.
ridhika, ku-, v.i. be pleased, be content.
rijali, n. man with sexual powers.
rika, ma-, n. people of the same age, age group.
rimbwata, n. love medicine to affect a male companion.
rindima, ku-, v.i. rumble.
ringa, ku-, v.i. boast, put on airs.

ripea   rukwa

ripea, ku-, v.t. repair, mend, *ripea viatu,* mend shoes.
ripoti, n. report.
risala, n. oration, *soma risala,* read a speech.
risasi, n. bullet, *piga risasi,* shoot (gun).
risiti, n. receipt.
rithi, ku-, v.t. inherit, *rithi utajiri,* inherit wealth.
riwaya, n. novel, school of thought.
rizavu, n. reserve.
riziki, n. outcome of one's work for one's survival.
robo, n. quarter (1/4), *robo kilo,* 1/4 kg.
robota, ma-, n. bale, bundle.
roda, n. pulley.
roga, ku-, v.t. bewitch.
roho, n. soul, spirit, *toa roho,* kill.
rojorojo, adj. pasty, thick, viscous, heavy soup.
ropoka, ku-, v.i. talk nonsense.
rozari, n. rosary.
ruba, n. leech.
rubani, ma-, n. pilot.
rubega, n. man's open sided cloak especially worn by pastoralistic people.
rubuni, ku-, v.t. cheat cleverly, to convince through clever language so as to obtain favour.
rudi, ku-, v.i. return, come back, *rudia,* repeat, *rudisha,* give back.
rudiana, ku-, v.t. reunite, replay.
rufaa, n. appeal, *kata rufaa,* to appeal (law court).
rufani, see **rufaa**.
rugaruga, ma-, n. mercenaries.
ruhusa, n. permission, *mpe ruhusa,* give him permission.
ruhusu, ku-, v.t. permit, allow, dismiss, *nakuruhusu kwenda nyumbani,* I allow you to go home.
ruka, ku-, v.i. jump, *ruka mstari,* jump a line.
rukia, ku-, v.t. jump at 2. interrupt, *usirukie maneno yetu,* don't interrupt our discussion cut in.
rukwa, ku-, v.i. *rukwa na*

153

rula

akili, lose one's head, be mentally deranged, lose one's senses.

rula, n. ruler, for drawing lines.

rumande, n. custody, remand.
run deep.

rundika, ku-, pile up.

rungu, n. club, a stick with a round head, cudgel, *fikiri sana*, cudgel one's brain.

rupia, n. rupee, *rupia tano*, five rupees.

ruzuku

rusha, ku-, v.t. throw up in the air.

rushia, ku-, v.t. throw something to somebody.

rushwa, n. bribe, *toa rushwa*, give a bribe, *pokea rushwa*, accept a bribe.

rutuba, n. fertility (of soil).

rutubisha, ku-, v.t. make fertile.

ruzuku, n. subsidy, *ruzuku ni haki ya kisiasa*, subsidy is a political right.

S

saa, n. watch 2. hour, *saa ngapi?* what is the time? *amevaa saa mpya*, he has a new watch.
saada, n. luck, goodluck.
saba, adj. seven (7).
sababisha, ku-, v.t. cause something, be the cause of.
sababu, n. cause, reason, *kwa sababu*, because of.
sabahi, ku-, v.t. greet (in the morning).
sabalkheri! interj. goodmorning.
sabasaba, n. Trade Fair Day in Tanzania.
sabato, n. sabbath day.
sabini, adj. seventy (70).
sabuni, n. soap.
sachi, ku-, v.t. search.
sadaka, n. sacrifice, alms, *toa sadaka*, give alms.
sadifu, ku-, v.i. happen simulteneously.
sadiki, ku-, v.i. believe, *je, unasadiki sasa?* do you believe now?
sadikika, ku-, v.t. be credible.

safari, n. trip, *fanya safari*, make a trip.
safariutengano, n. departure.
safi, adj. clean, *maji safi*, clean water.
safiri, ku-, v.i. travel.
safirisha, ku-, v.t. transport, send away.
safisha, ku-, v.t. cleanse, purify.
safishika, ku-, v.t. be cleansed, purified.
safura, n. disease caused by hookworms.
saga, ku-, v.t. grind,
sagika, ku-, v.t. be milled, be ground.
sagisha, ku-, v.t. have something ground.
sahani, n. plate.
sahau, ku-, v.i. forget, *usisahau*, don't forget.
sahaulifu, adj. forgetful, inattentive.
sahaulika, ku-, v.i. be forgotten.
sahaulisha, ku-, v.t. cause to forget.

sahaulivu — sanaa

sahaulivu, adj. forgetful.
sahibu, n. friend, companion.
sahihi, adj. correct.
sahihisha, ku-, v.t. correct mistakes.
sahili, ku-, v.t. simplify.
saidia, ku-, v.t. help, assist.
saidiana, ku-, v.i. cooperate.
saikolojia, n. psychology, *saikolojia ya elimu*, educational psychology.
saili, ku-, v.t. interrogate, interview.
saini, n. signature, 2. ku-, *tia saini*, sign.
sajili, ku-, v.t. register.
sajini, n. sergent.
saka, ku-, v.t. hunt down, fumble.
sakafia, ku-, v.t. cement.
sakafu, n. floor, *sakafia*, put a floor.
sakama, ku-, v.t. press somebody for something, insist.
sakata, ku-, v.t. hit, 2. n.fracas, pushing and shoving during a commotion.
sala, n. prayer.
salama, adj. safe 2. adv. safely, *fika salama*, have a nice trip, bon voyage.
salamu, n. greetings, *salamu zao*, greetings to them.
sali, ku-, v.i. pray, *twende kusali*, let's go to pray.
salia, ku-, v.i. remain, be left over.
salimia, salimu, ku-, v.t. greet, *je, amekusalimia*, or *amekusalimu?* has he greeted you?
salimini, adv. safely, *salama salimini*, safely.
saliti, ku-, v.t. betray, be disloyal.
samaki, n. fish.
samawati, n. azure.
sambaa, ku-, v.i. spread, disperse.
sambamba na, adj. parallel to.
sambaza, ku-, v.t. spread, etc.
sambusa, n. samosa.
samehe, ku-, v.t. forgive.
sampuli, n. sample.
sana, adv. much, very, *safi sana*, very clean, very good.
sanaa, n. art.

sanamu · semea

sanamu, n. image, idol.
sanda, n. shroud, burial cloth.
sandali, n. sandal-wood.
sandarusi, n. resin.
sanduku, ma-, n. box.
sangara, n. Nile perch, small red ant.
sanifisha, ku-, v.t. standardize.
sanifu, adj. standard, *Kiswahili sanifu*, standard Kiswahili.
sanii, ku-, v.t. produce an art work.
santuri, n. gramaphone.
sanzua, ku-, v.t. remove without permission.
sarafu, n. coin.
sarakani, n. cancer (disease).
sarakasi, n. circuss.
sare, n. uniform 2. draw (in a game).
saruji, n. cement, concrete.
sasa, adv. now, *sasa hivi*, just now.
sato, n. grey tilapia.
saumu, n. abstinence, fasting, garlic.
sauti, n. voice, sound.
savana, n. savannah.

sawa, adj. equal to, *hii ni sawa na ile*, this is equal to that.
sawasawa, adv. correctly, equally.
sawazisha, ku-, v.t. level out 2. equalise, counterbalance.
sawijika, ku-, v.i. be emaciated.
sayansi, n. science.
sayari, n. planet.
saza, ku-, v.t. leave something over, have more than needed.
sebule, n. verandah, living room.
sefu, n. safe.
sehemu, n. section, part.
sekeneko, n. syphilis.
sekenene, n. eyelid pimple.
sekunde, n. second.
seli, n. cell, sale.
sema, ku-, v.t. speak out, say.
semansi, n. summons.
sembe n. maize flour.
sembuse, adv. let alone.
semea, ku-, v.t. accuse (used by children), *nitakusemea kwa mama*, I will accuse you to mother.

semekana, ku-, v.i. be purported.
semesha, ku-, v.t. speak to.
semina, n. seminar, *shiriki semina*, attend a seminar.
seminari, n. seminary, *seminari kuu*, major seminary.
senene, n. green grasshopper.
seng'enge, n. wire used to enclose a compound.
sengenya, ku-, v.t. slander, backbite.
sensa, n. census.
sentafowadi, n. centerforward.
sentensi, n. sentence, *tunga sentensi*, make a sentence.
sentigramu, n. centigramme.
sentimita, n. centimetre.
sepetuka, ku-, v.i. falter.
septemba, n. september.
sera, n. policy.
seremala, n. carpenter.
serereka, ku-, v.i. slide, skid.
serikali, n. government, *serikali ya mpito*, transitional government.
shaba, n. brass, copper.
shabaha, n. aim, intention, target, *lenga shabaha*, take aim.
shabashi! interj. wonderful, wow!
shada, ma-, n. cluster.
shaghalabaghala, adv. haphazardly.
shahada, n. degree, *shahada ya pili*, Master's Degree.
shahawa, n. sperms, semen.
shahidi, ma-, n. witness.
shaibu, n. very old man.
shairi, ma-, n. poem, poetry, *tunga shairi*, compose a poem.
shajara, n. diary.
shajaraasili, n. geneaology.
shaka, ma-, n. doubt, *hamna shaka*, no doubt.
shamba, ma-, n. farm, plantation, countryside.
shambulia, ku-, v.t. attack, invade, assault.
shambulio, ma-, n. attack, assault.
shamiri, ku-, v.i. prosper.
shamrashamra, n.

shanga

celebrations, gaiety.
shanga, n. beads.
shangaa, ku-, v.i. be amazed, be surprised, wonder.
shangaza, ku-, v.t. astonish, cause amazement.
shangazi, n. aunt, *shangazi yako*, your aunt.
shangilia, ku-, v.t. applaud by clapping hands and singing.
shangingi, n. experienced prostitute (street language, not standard Swahili).
shangwe, n. rejoicing, festivity, *fanya shangwe*, rejoice.
shani, n. novelty, adventure.
shanta, n. rucksack.
shanuo, n. comb.
sharabu, ku-, v.t. absorb, drink up.
shari, n. ill luck, evil tendency.
sharti, ma-, n. condition necessary for something (also **sherti, shurti**).
sharubu, n. moustache.

shenzi

shatashata, adj. juicy, rich food, rich soup.
shati, ma-, n. shirt.
shauku, n. strong desire, enthusiasm.
shauri, ma-, n. advice, consultation, *fanya shauri*, consult with somebody.
shauriana, ku-, v.i. consult one another.
shavu, ma-, n. cheek, *busu shavuni*, kiss on the check, *shavu la samaki*, gill.
shawishi, ku-, v.t. tempt, entice.
shawishika, ku-, v.i. be tempted.
shayiri, n. barley.
sheha, n. headman.
shehe, ma-, n. sheikh (s).
shehena, n. cargo, freight, shipment.
sheheneza, ku-, v.t. load cargo.
sheheni, ku-, v.t. be loaded with cargo.
shemasi, ma-, n. deacon(s).
shemeji, ma-, n. brother-in-law or sister-in-law.
shenzi, adj. uncivilized,

rude, uncouth.
shere, n. ridicule, derision.
sherehe, n. celebration.
sherehekea, ku-, v.t. celebrate.
sheria, n. law, *mwanasheria*, lawyer.
shetani, n. devil, satan.
shiba, ku-, v.i. eat enough, be satisfied.
shibe, n. satiation.
shibisha, ku-, v.t. give enough food.
shida, n. hardship, *kwa shida*, with difficulty.
shifti, n. shift.
shika, ku-, v.t. hold, take.
shikamana, ku-, v.i. stick together, unite, cohere.
shikamoo, n. greetings to older people, who answer, *marahaba*.
shikilia, ku-, v.t. hold.
shikio, n. handle, something to hold by.
shime, n. encouragement, *nipe shime*, help me.
shimizi, n. petticoat, chemise.
shimo, ma-, n. hole.
shina, ma-, n. trunk, source.
shindana, ku-, v.i. compete with.
shindania, ku-, v.t. compete for.
shindano, ma-, n. competition.
shindika, ku-, v.t. close, shut.
shindilia, ku-, n. cram, press.
shingo, n. neck, *ana shingo ndefu*, she is long necked.
shinikiza, ku-, v.t. pressurize.
shinikizo, n. pressure, *shinikizo la damu*, blood pressure.
shirika, ma-, n. cooperative.
shiriki, ku-, v.i. take part in.
shirikiana, ku-, v.i. work together, cooperate.
shirikisha, ku-, v.t. involve, include, associate.
shitaka, ma-, n. accusation.
shitaki, ku-, v.t. accuse, *wanashitakiwa kwa ubakaji*, they are accused of rape.
shitua, ku-, v.t. shock.

shoga   shusha

shoga, ma-, n. friend (between women) 2. **ma-,** n. a homosexual, gay.
shokoa, n. forced labour.
shombe, n. halfcaste, mulatto, mixed blood person.
shombo, n. fish smell.
shomoro, n. sparrow.
shona, ku-, v.t. sew, mend by sewing.
shonea, ku-, v.t. sew for, sew on.
shonesha, ku-, v.t. have a dress made.
shoti, n. loss.
shoto, n. left hand, left side.
shtaki, see **shitaki**.
shtua, see **shitua**.
shtuka, ku-, v.i. get a shock, be startled.
shtusha, ku-, v.i. shock, startle.
shubiri, n. bitter aloe.
shufaa, n. forgiveness, pardon.
shufwa, n. even number.
shughuli, n. business, work, special activity.
shughulika, ku-, v.i. be busy.
shughulisha, ku-, v.t. occupy, give work to.
shuhudia, ku-, v.i. witness, corroborate.
shujaa, ma-, n. hero.
shuka, ku-, v.i. descend 2. n. shuka, bedsheet.
shukia, ku-, v.i. descend on.
shukrani, n. thanks, gratitude.
shuku, ku-, v.t. suspect, *unamshuku nani?* whom do you suspect?
shukuru, ku-, v.t. give thanks.
shule, n. school, *enda shule,* go to school, *shule ya chekechea,* nursery school.
shume, n. wild cat.
shupaa, ku-, v.i. be obstinate.
shupavu, adj. firm, brave.
shupaza, n. spades in playing cards 2. **ku-,** harden, make obstinate.
shurtisho, n. compulsion.
shuruti, n. necessity, obligatory.
shurutisha, ku-, v.t. force somebody to do something, compel.
shusha, ku-, v.t. bring down.

shushua — simama

shushua, ku-, v.t. put to shame, expose.
shushushu, n. intelligence officer, spy.
shutuma, n. accusation, blame, criticism.
shutumiwa, ku-, v.t. be accused of.
shutumu, ku-, v.t. blame.
shwari, adj. calm, peaceful.
si, adv. of negation, is not, are not, is not, *yeye si mwizi*, he is not a thief, *mimi si mwalimu*, I am not a teacher.
siafu, n. red brown ants, safari ants.
siagi, n. butter.
siasa, n. politics, science and art of government, *John anapenda siasa*, John is interested in politics.
siborio, n. ciborium.
sidiria, n. brassiere.
sifa, n. praise, reputation, qualification.
sifika, ku-, v.i. be renowned for something.
sifongo, n. sponge.
sifu, ku-, v.t. praise, *msifu Bwana*, praise the Lord.
sifuri, n. zero, nil, nought.
sigara, n. cigarette.
siha, n. health.
sihi, ku-, v.t. entreat, beseech.
sijambo, adv. I am well.
siki, n. vinegar.
sikia, ku-, v.i. hear.
sikika, ku-, v.i. be audible.
sikiliza, ku-, v.t. listen.
sikilizana, ku-, v.i. to be in agreement.
sikio, ma-, n. ear, *tega sikio*, listen carefully.
sikitika, ku-, v.i. be sorry, sad.
sikitikia, ku-, v.t. deplore.
sikitiko, ma-, n. sorrow, grief.
sikivu, adj. obedient, attentive.
siku, n. day, *siku zote*, always; *siku kwa siku*, day after day.
silabasi, n. syllabus.
silabi, n. syllable.
silaha, n. arms, weapon.
silesi, n. slice of bread.
silika, n. instinct.
silimu, ku-, v.i. be converted ot Islam.
silinda, n. cylinder.
simama, ku-, v.i. stand up

simamia   sisimka

2. stop.
simamia, ku-, v.t. supervise.
simamisha, ku-, v.t. raise up 2. to cause the penis to be erect.
simanga, ku-, v.t. reproach.
simango, n. reproach, jeers.
simanzi, n. grief, depression.
simba, n. lion, *watoto wa simba*, lion's cubs, *simba jike*, lioness.
simbi, n. cowrie.
simbika, ku-, v.t. entangle thread on a fishing hook.
simbiko, n. entanglement.
sime, n. knife (of large size).
simika, ku-, v.t. erect, set up, enthrone.
simile, interj. step aside, make way!
simsim, n. sesame.
simu, n. telephone, *simu ya mkononi*, mobile phone, 2. telegram.
simulia, ku-, v.t. narrate, relate.
simulizi, ma-, n. narration.
sinasina, ku-, v.i. cry silently.
sindano, n. needle, *piga sindano*, give an injection.
sindika, ku-, v.t. extract, shut, close.
sindikiza, ku-, v.t. see a guest off, accompany, escort.
singa, n. long straight hair 2. **ku-,** v.t. massage, rub with oil or perfume.
singe, n. bayonet.
singizia, ku-, v.t. lay blame on, slander; *jisingizia*, pretend.
sinia, ma-, n. platter.
sinodi, n. synod.
sinyaa, ku-, v.i. wither away, waste away.
sinzia, ku-, v.t. be sleepy, doze.
siri, n. secret, *kwa siri*, secretly.
siriba, ku-, v.t. plaster, spread liquid substance on sth/sb.
sisi, per. pron. we, *sisi sote*; all of us.
sisimizi, n. black ant.
sisimka, ku-, v.i. tingle with excitement, fear or cold.

sisimua, ku-, v.t. stimulate, excite.
sisitiza, ku-, v.t. insist upon.
sista, ma-, n. nun.
sita, also **sitasita, ku-,** v.t. hesitate, be doubtful; 2. n. six.
sitawi, ku-, v.i. prosper, flourish, progress.
sitawisha, ku-, v.t. grow (plants).
sitiari, n. metaphor.
sitini, adj. sixty.
sitiri, ku-, v.t. preserve, keep secret.
sivyo, adv. not so.
siyo, adv. not.
soda, n. soda.
sofa, n. sofa.
soga, n. chat, *piga soga,* to engage in light entertaining chat.
sogea, ku-, v.i. move closer, make room.
sogelea, ku-, v.t. move closer to somebody.
sogeza, ku-, v.t. push something nearer to or a little distance, push.
soka, n. soccer.
soketi, n. socket.
soko, ma-, n. market.
sokomeza, ku-, v.t. push into a small space, stuff inside.
sokomoko, n. confusion, turmoil.
sokota, ku-, v.t. weave, spin.
soksi, n. socks.
sokwe, ma-, n. ape.
sokwemtu, n. chimpanzee.
soli, n. shoes' sole.
soma, ku-, v.t. read.
somba, ku-, v.t. move things from one place to another.
somea, ku-, v.t. study for something, *anasomea nini*? what is he studying for?
someka, ku-, v.i. be readable.
somesha, ku-, v.t. teach 2. sponsor a student.
somo, ma-, n. lesson, *mpe somo,* give him a lesson.
songa, ku-, v.t. press close 2. v. process of cooking ugali (stiff porridge).
songamana, ku-, v.i. be crowded, jostle each other.
soni, n. disgrace, shyness.
sonya, n. whistle in contempt.

soseji

soseji, n. sausage.
sosiolojia, n. sociology.
sote, pron. *sisi sote*, all of us.
sotoka, n rinderpest.
spana, n. spanner.
spea, n. sparepart.
spidi, n. speed.
stadi, adj. skilful, expert.
stahi, ku-, v.t. respect, esteem.
stahiki, ku-, v.i. deserve, be worthy.
stahili, ku-, v.t. deserve, merit.
stahimili, ku-, v.t. endure.
staili, n. style, see **mtindo**.
stakabadhi, n. receipt.
starehe, n. enjoyment, comfort 2. answer to karibu (welcome).
stesheni, n. station.
stima, n. steamer, gas cooker.
stoo, n. store.
stovu, n. stove.
studio, n. studio.
stuli, n. stool.
subira, n. patience, *subira yavuta heri*, patience pays.
subiri, ku-, v.t. wait for somebody or something.

sukus

subu, n. mould.
sudi, n. luck.
sufi, n. wool.
sufii, n. hermit, dervish.
sufu, n. wool.
sufuria, n. cooking pot, pan.
sugu, n. callosity, callousness; *yu sugu*, he is obstinate, hardened.
sugua, ku-, v.t. rub, scrub.
suhubiana, ku-, v.i. flirt, *mpanda pikipiki alisuhubiana na kifo*, a motorcyclist flirted with death.
sujudia, ku-, v.t. bow to, bow before, genuflect.
sujudu, ku-, v.t. bow in reverence.
suka, ku-, v.t. twist, *suka nywele*, plait the hair.
sukari, n. sugar.
sukasuka, ku-, v.t. agitate.
sukuma, ku-, v.t. push.
sukuma-wiki, n. rape plant.
sukumia, ku-, v.t. push toward, *sukumiza*, drive on, forward.
sukumiza, ku-, v.t. push, shove.
sukus, n. a dance music of Congolese origin.

sukutua   swila

sukutua, ku-, v.t. rinse out the mouth with water, gargle.
sulibisha, ku-, v.t. crucify also **sulubisha**.
sulisuli, n. type of kingfish.
suluhisha, ku-, v.t. reconcile.
suluhisho, n. reconciliation, mediation, solution.
suluhu, adv. draw.
sumaku, n. magnet.
sumbua, ku-, v.t. trouble, bother.
sumbufu, adj. troublesome, *mbona wewe msumbufu hivyo?* why are you so troublesome? irksome.
sumbuka, ku-, v.i. suffer, be troubled.
sumbuko, ma-, n. trouble
sumbwi, n. fist thrown at somebody.
sumu, n. poison, toxin.
suna, n. commendable deed.
sungura, n. rabbit, hare.
sungusungu, n. black ant, militia, home guard.
suni, n. sunnite sect.

supu, n. soup.
sura, n. face, appearance 2. n. chapter, lesson.
suria, ma-, n. mistress, concubine.
suriama, n. halfcaste, mixed blood.
surua, n. measles, *anaugua surua*, she/he is suffering from measles.
suruali, n. pair of trousers.
surupwete, n. valueless clothes.
susa, susia, v.t. boycott.
susu, n. hammock.
suta, ku-, v.t. refute, allege, confront, expose, *suta mwizi*, confront, expose a thief.
suuza, ku-, v.t. rinse, swill.
swaga, ku-, v.t. drive cattle.
swahibu, n. friend, *swahibu wangu ameaga dunia*, my beloved friend has passed away.
swala, n. gazelle, prayer.
swali, ma-, n. question 2. **ku-,** v.i. to pray (especially for Moslems).
sweta, n. sweater.
swichi, n. switch.
swila, n. hammock, spitting cobra.

T

taa, n. lamp; *washa taa*, light a lamp; *zima taa*, put out a lamp.
taabani, adv. in bad condition.
taabika, ku-, v.i. suffer, be in distress.
taabisha, ku-, v.t. trouble, cause suffering.
taabu, n. worry, distress, trouble.
taadhima, n. respect, *kwa heshima na taadhima*, with all due respect.
taahira, n. mentally retarded.
taaluma, n. profession.
taamuli, n. meditation.
taarabu, n. music with origin and melody of East African coast.
taarifa, n. information, message.
taasisi, n. institute.
tabaka, ma-, n. layer, stratum, social class, *tabaka la juu*, upper class.
tabaruku, ku-, v.i. bless, congregate together for prayer.
tabasamu, ku-, v.i. smile.
tabenakulo, n. tabernacle.
tabia, n. nature, conduct; *ana tabia nzuri*, he is well behaved, good mannered.
tabibu, n. healer, doctor.
tabiri, ku-, v.t. forecast, foretell.
tabu, n. distress, misery.
tadi, ku-, v.t. transgress, offend.
tafadhali, adv. please.
tafadhalisha, ku-, v.t. request kindly.
tafakari, ku-, v.i. think, meditate.
tafiti, ku-, v.t. investigate, research.
tafrija, n. party, *andaa tafrija*, give a party.
tafsida, n. veiled language, euphemism.
tafsiri, ku-, v.t. translate.
tafuna, ku-, v.t. chew, (fig) *ametafuna fedha za umma*, he has squandered public funds.

tafuta   **tamaa**

tafuta, ku-, v.t. look for, search for.
taga, ku-, v.t. lay eggs.
tahadhari, n. precaution, care, *tahadhari kabla ya shari*, precaution before danger.
tahakiki, n. review, critique.
tahamaki, ku-, v.i. be upset.
tahariri, n. editorial comments.
taharuki, n. excitement, anxiety.
tahayuri, n. humiliation.
tahini, ku-, v.t. test, examine.
tahiri, ku-, v.t. circumcise, *baada ya siku nane alitahiriwa*, after eight days, he was circumcised.
tai, n. eagle 2. tie.
taifa, ma-, n. nation.
taifisha, ku-, v.t. nationalize.
taifodi, n. typhoid.
tairi, n. tyre.
taja, ku-, v.t. mention.
taji, n. crown.
tajiri, ma-, n. rich person.
tajirika, ku-, v.i. become rich.

tajirisha, ku-, v.t. enrich, make somebody rich.
taka, ku-, v.t. want, wish.
takasa, ku-, v.t. purify, cleanse.
takata, ku-, v.i. be clean, be purified.
takataka, n. rubbish, garbage, filth, waste.
takatifu, adj. holy, *nchi takatifu*, holy land.
takia, ku-, v.t. wish somebody something, *nakutakia heri*, I wish you all the best.
tako, ma-, n. buttocks.
takribani, adv. almost, about.
takrima, n. reception hospitality.
taksiri, n. crime.
takwimu, n. statistics, *Idara ya Takwimu*, Statistics Bureau.
talaka, n. divorce.
talii, ku-, v.i. tour (as tourist), peruse.
taliki, ku-, v.t. give a divorce.
tama, n. cheek.
tamaa, n. lust, desire, *fanya tamaa*, desire; *kata tamaa*, despair.

tamalaki, ku-, v.i. rule, exercise authority.
tamani, ku-, v.t. desire, wish, covet.
tamanisha, ku-, v.t. entice.
tamasha, n. show, concert, *tamasha la muziki,* a music concert.
tamathali, n. figure of speech.
tamati, n. conclusion, end.
tamba, ku-, v.i. boast, brag.
tambaa, ku-, v.i. crawl, creep, *mimea inayotambaa,* creeping plants.
tambarare, n. plain, even, level.
tambaza, ku-, v.t. drawl.
tambika, ku-, v.i. make offerings to the ancestors, to conduct rituals.
tambiko, n. sacrifice to the ancestors, ancestral rituals.
tambo, n. amplitude.
tambua, ku-, v.t. recognise, identify, *nimekutambua kwa sauti yako,* I have recognised you by your voice.
tambulisha, ku-, v.t. introduce somebody, or introduce something (new).
tambuu, n. betel leaf.
tamka, ku-, v.t. pronounce, utter some words.
tamko, ma-, n. pronouncement, declaration.
tamshi, ma-, n. see **tamko,** 2. pronunciation.
tamthilia, n. drama, play.
tamu, adj. sweet, delicious, *chakula kitamu,* delicious meal.
tanabahi, ku-, v.i. realize, become aware.
tanabahisha, ku-, v.t. alert someone, remind.
tanbihi, n. footnote, endnote, notabene, note.
tanda, ku-, v.t. spread out.
tandaza, ku-, v.t. spread something out.
tandika, ku-, v.t. arrange something; *tandika kitanda,* make a bed.
tandiko, ma-, n. bedding, mattress.
tandu, n. centipede.
tangamana, ku-, v.i. mix, be together.

tangamano, n. togetherness, harmony.
tangatanga, ku-, v.i. wander about, walk aimlessly.
tangawizi, n. ginger.
tangaza, ku-, v.t. announce, make public, *tangaza redioni*, announce on the radio.
tangazo, ma-, n. notice, publication, *tangazo la biashara*, commercial advertisement.
tangi, ma-, n. tank (of water).
tango, ma-, n. cucumber.
tangu, prep. since, *tangu jana*, since yesterday.
tangua, ku-, v.t. abolish, annul, declare as invalid, cancel.
tangulia, ku-, v.i. go infront, be ahead, precede.
tani, n. ton.
tania, ku-, v.t. make fun of, tease, joke with.
tano, adj. five (5).
tanua, ku-, v.t. expand, dilate.
tanuka, ku-, v.i. wide open, extend, expand.

tanuru, ma-, n. brick-kiln, furnace.
tanzi, n. loop, slipknot.
tanzia, n. death news.
tanzu, n. branch.
tanzua, ku-, v.t. solve a problem/puzzle.
tanzuka, ku-, v.i. be solved, be clarified.
tapakaa, ku-, v.i. be scattered all over.
tapanya, ku-, v.t. scatter about, *tapanya fedha*, squander money, disspate.
tapatapa, ku-, v.i. be unsure, confused, struggle to survive, flounder.
tapeli, ma-, n. , conman, trickster, cheat(s) 2. v.t. ku-, to cheat, to con.
tapika, ku-, v.t. vomit.
tapisha, ku-, v.t. flash something in toilet.
tarabushi, n. fez.
tarafa, n. county, division.
taraji, ku-, v.t. hope, intend.
tarajia, ku-, v.i. expect, hope for.
tarajio, ma-, n. expectation, *nini*

tarakimu   tayarisha

matarajio yako ya baadaye? what are your future expectations?

tarakimu, n. numeral.

taratibu, n. order 2. adv. orderly, procedures.

tarehe, n. date.

tarishi, ma-, n. messenger.

tarumbeta, ma-, n. trampet.

tasa, adj. barren, impotent, sterile, *mwanamke tasa*, a barren woman 2. n. odd number.

tasbihi, n. prayer beads held together by a chain or thread.

tashwishi, n. doubt, uncertainity.

taslimu, n. cash, *fedha taslimu,* cash.

taswira, n. pictue, image.

tatanisha, ku-, v.t. confuse, clog, confound.

tatanua, ku-, v.t. disentangle.

tatarika, ku-, v.i. rattle, crackle.

tathmini, ku-, v.t. evaluate.

tatiza, ku-, v.i. elude.

tatizo, ma-, n. problem.

tatu, adj. three (3).

tatua, ku-, v.t. solve, resolve.

tauhidi, n. theology.

taulo, n. towel.

tauni, n. plague.

tausi, n. peacock, *uzuri wa tausi,* peacock's beauty.

tawa, ku-, v.i. live in seclusion.

tawadha, ku-, v.i. make ablutions just before prayers (Moslems), wash after defeacating.

tawala, ku-, v.t. rule, govern, dominate.

tawanya, ku-, v.t. scatter, diffuse.

tawanyika, ku-, v.i. disperse, go away, be scattered.

tawaza, ku-, v.t. instal as ruler.

tawi, ma-, n. branch, *fungua tawi jipya,* open a new branch.

taya, ma-, n. cheek-bone, jaw.

tayari, adj. ready, *kila kitu tayari,* everything is ready.

tayarisha, ku-, v.t.

tazama — tendea

prepare, make ready.
tazama, ku-, v.t. look at.
tazamia, ku-, v.i. expect, hope for.
tega, ku-, v.t. set a trap, *tega sikio*, listen.
tegemea, ku-, v.t. depend on, expect on.
tegemeo, ma-, n. expectation, support.
tegemeza, ku-, v.t. support with.
tegemezi, n. dependant.
tego, n. maguni, ailment to punish those who practise adultery.
tegua, ku-, v.t. let go, *tegua mtego*, let a trap go off 2. strain a limb.
teguka, ku-, v.i. be sprained.
teka, ku-, v.t. draw, *teka maji*, draw water 2. n. ma-, captive, *chukua mateka*, take captive(s).
teke, ma-, n. kick, *piga teke*, kick, tender and soft.
tekeleza, ku-, v.t. fulfil, implement, excute.
tekelezo, n. excution, implementation.
tekenya, ku-, v.t. tickle.

teketeke, adj. soft, very tender.
teketeza, ku-, v.t. consume, devastate.
tele, adj. abundant.
telekeza, ku-, v.t. abandon, *ametelekeza familia yake*, he has abandoned his family.
telemsha, teremsha, ku-, v.t. let down something, cause to descend.
tema, ku-, v.t. spit out, eject out.
tembea, ku-, v.i. walk, go about, *tembea kwa miguu*, walk on foot.
tembelea, ku-, v.t. visit.
tembeza, ku-, v.t. walk a person 2. *tembeza biashara*, hawk something.
tembo, n. elephant 2. palm wine.
tena, adv. again.
tenda, ku-, v.i. act 2. tender.
tende, n. date (fruit), **ma-,** n. elephantiasis (disease).
tendea, ku-, v.t. do something to somebody; *amekutendea nini?* what

tenga

has he done to you?
tenga, ku-, v.t. set aside something for a purpose 2. **ma-,** n. a basket made of bamboo sticks.
tengana, ku-, v.i. separate from each other.
tenganisha, ku-, v.t. disconnect.
tengemaa, ku-, v.i. be complete, be in order.
tengeneza, ku-, v.t. make, repair.
tengenezo, ma-, n. repair.
tengua, ku-, v.t. nullify, cancel, *mahakama imetengua hukumu ya kifo,* the court has nullified the death penalty.
teremka, ku-, v.i come down, disembark (from a vessel), descend.
teremsha, ku-, v.t. set something down, bring down from above.
tesa, ku-, v.t. persecute, afflict, (sl) enjoy oneself.
teseka, ku-, v.i. suffer, *watoto wanateseka,* children are suffering.
teso, ma-, n. suffering, affliction.

thawabu

teta, ku-, v.t. backbite, slander.
tetea, ku-, v.t. defend, plead for, *tetea taji,* defend the title.
tetema, ku-, v.i. shake (from cold, fever or fear).
tetemeka, ku-, v.i. tremble (from cold or fear).
tetemeko, ma-, n. earthquake, *tetemeko laua mamia ya watu,* an earthquake kills hundreds of people.
tetesi, n. rumour, hearsay.
teto, ma-, n. slander, gossip.
teua, ku-, v.t. appoint, select, *Rais ameteua mabalozi,* the president has appointed ambassadors.
teule, adj. selected, holy, eligible.
tezi, n. goitre, glandular.
thabiti, adj. firm.
thamani, n. value, *kodi ya ongezeko la thamani,* value added tax.
thamini, n. value, esteem.
thawabu, n. a reward expected from God in

the next life for one's good deeds here on earth.
thelathini, adj. thirty.
theluji, n. snow, *tembea kwenye theluji*, walk on snow.
theluthi, adj. one-third.
themanini, adj. eighty (80).
themometa, n. thermometer.
thenashara, n. twelve.
theolojia, n. theology.
thibitisha, ku-, v.t. prove, give evidence, approve, affirm.
thibitisho, n. confirmation, proof.
thubutu, ku-, v.i. dare, venture.
thumni, adj. fifty cents 2. n. something divided into eight equal parts.
tia, ku-, v.t. put in, *tia sukari*, put in sugar.
tiara, n. crown.
tia-saini, ku-, v.t. endorse.
tiba, n. cure; *UKIMWI hauna tiba*, AIDS has no cure, *kinga ni bora kuliko tiba*, prevention is better than cure.

tibu, ku-, v.t. treat medically.
tibua, ku-, v.t. stir up, arouse.
tifua, ku-, v.t. stir up, dig out, plough, *tifua ardhi*, plough the land.
tifutifu, adj. dusty, soil in between sandy and clay.
tii, ku-, v.t. obey, *tiifu*, adj. obedient.
tiifu, adj. obedient, submissive.
tijara, n. surplus, profit.
tiketi, n. ticket.
tikisa, ku-, v.t. shake, *tikisa nchi*, shake the nation.
tikisika, ku-, v.i. be shaken.
tikiti, ma-, n. watermelon.
timamu, adj. normal, sane.
timbi, n. bracelet.
timia, ku-, v.i. be complete.
timilifu, adj. perfect.
timiza, ku-, v.t. fulfil, carry out, *timiza ahadi*, fulfil a promise, accomplish.
timu, n. team.
tindikali, n. acid.

tindikiwa

tindikiwa, ku-, v.i. be short of, *tumetindikiwa dawa,* we are short of medicine.
tindo, n. chisel.
tingatinga, n. marsh area, bridge made of timber.
tipwatipwa, adj. soft and plump.
tiririka, ku-, v.i. flow, truckle.
tisa, adj. nine (9)
tisha, ku-, v.t. frighten, scare. **tishio, ma-,** v. threat(s).
tishika, ku-, v.i. be terrified.
tishio, n. threat.
tisini, adj. ninety (90).
titi, ma-, n. nipple of breast, teat.
toa, ku-, v.t. give, to produce, to take out, consign.
toba, n. repentance.
tobo, ma-, n. hole.
toboa, ku-, v.t. bore a hole through.
toboka, ku-, v.i. be bored through, have a hole.
tochi, n. torch.
tofali, ma-, n. brick.
tofauti, n. difference,

tolea

hamna tofauti, no difference; *iko tofauti,* there is a difference.
tofautiana, ku-, v.i. differ.
tofautisha, ku-, v.t. differentiate.
tohara, n. circumcision, *tohara ya wanawake ni hatari,* women circumcision is dangerous.
tohoa, ku-, v.t. coin new words.
toka, ku-, v.i. come out, go out; *toka nje,* go outside; *tokea hapo,* since then.
tokea, ku-, v.i. appear 2. come from; *unatokea wapi?* where are you coming from?
tokeo, ma-, n. occurrance, results, outcome, score.
tokeza, ku-, v.i. stick out, appear.
tokomea, ku-, v.i. disappear, eliminate.
tokomeza, ku-, v.t. destroy totally, decimate.
tokota, ku-, v.i. boil.
tolea, ku-, v.t. offer something; *tolea sadaka,* offer sacrifice.

tolewa

tolewa, ku-, v.t. be offered.
tomasa, ku-, v.t. press gently.
tomba, ku-, v.t. have sex, fuck, copulate.
tombana, ku-, v.t. have sex with, fuck with.
tombola, n. lottery, tombola.
tombwa, ku-, v.t. be fucked.
tomoko, ma-, n. custard-apple.
tomondo, ma-, n. malay-apple.
tone, ma-, n. drop.
tonesha, ku-, v.t. touch a sore place, revive the pain.
tonge, ma-, n. ball of food.
tongo, ma-, n. discharge from eye.
tongoa, ku-, v.t. explain clearly with examples.
tongoza, ku-, v.t. seduce a woman or man.
tope, ma-, n. mud.
topetope, ma-, n. custard-apple.
topu, adv. filled to the full.

tua

Torati, n. Torah, the first five books of the Bible.
toridhia, ku-, v.t. disapprove.
toroka, ku-, v.i. run away, escape.
toroli, ma-, n. trolley, wheelbarrow.
tosa, ku-, v.t. plunge into.
tosha, ku-, v.i. be enough.
tosheka, ku-, v.i. be satisfied.
tosheleza, ku-, v.t. satisfy needs.
totama, ku-, v.i. squat.
totoa, ku-, v.t. hatch out.
totoro, adv. complete darkness.
tovu, adv. mannerless.
towashi, ma-, n. eunuch.
toweka, ku-, v.i. disappear, vanish.
toza, ku-, v.t. levy, taxes.
transfoma, n. transformer.
trekta, ma-, n. tractor.
trela, ma-, n. trailler.
treni, n. train.
tropiki, n. tropic, *nchi za tropiki*, tropical countries.
tu, adv. only, just.
tua, ku-, v.t. land; *ndege imetua*, the bird has

landed, the aircraft has landed.
tuama, ku-, v.i. precipitate.
tubu, ku-, v.t. repent, feel remorse.
tufaha, ma-, n. apple.
tufani, n. hurricane, storm, typhoon.
tufe, ma-, n. globe (shape of planet earth).
tuhuma, n. suspicion, allegation, *tuhuma dhidi yake*, allegations against him.
tuhumiwa, ku-, v.i. be suspected.
tuhumu, ku-, v.t. suspect.
tui, n. coconut milk.
tukana, ku-, v.t. insult, abuse.
tukia, ku-, v.i. happen.
tukio, ma-, n. event, occasion.
tukufu, adj. glorious, full of glory.
tukuka, ku-, v.i. be exalted.
tukutu, m-, adj. naughty, mischievous.
tulia, ku-, v.i. be calm, be quiet.
tulivu, adj. peaceful.

tuliza, ku-, v.t. console, appease.
tulizana, ku-, v.t. comfort one another.
tulizo, n. consolation, comfort.
tuma, ku-, v.t. send, *tuma barua*, send a letter.
tumaini, ku-, v.t. to hope 2. n. hope, *tumaini jema*, good hope.
tumba, n. kind of long drum.
tumbaku, n. tobacco.
tumbili, n. monkey.
tumbo, ma-, n. stomach, *maumivu ya tumbo*, stomachache, abdominal pain.
tumbua, ku-, v.t. cut open.
tumbuiza, ku-, v.t. entertain, *tumbuiza watazamaji*, entertain the audience.
tumbuizo, n. entertainment.
tumbukia, ku-, v.i. fall into a hole.
tumbukiza, ku-, v.t. push into, drop into something.
tume, n. commission, *tume ya rais*,

tumia — twisha

presidential commission.
tumia, ku-, v.t. use, employ, utilize.
tumika, ku-, v.i. be used.
tumikia, ku-, v.t. serve.
tumikisha, ku-, v.t. make someone work for you.
tuna, ku-, v.i. puff out, swell out.
tunda, ma-, n. fruit.
tundika, ku-, v.t. hang.
tundu, ma-, n. hole.
tunga, ku-, v.t. compose; *tunga kitabu*, write a book.
tungika, ku-, v.t. hang up, suspend.
tungo, n. composition, essay.
tungua, ku-, v.t. take down, shoot down.
tunguja, n. small roundish tomato.
tunguri, n. witchdoctor's gourd.
tunukia, ku-, v.t. award.
tunza, ku-, v.t. take care, protect, guard 2. attend to, observe, give a gift to someone for one's good deed.
tunzo, n. reward, award, prize, *mshindi wa tunzo la Nobel*, Nobel Prize winner, honorarium..
tupa, ku-, v.t. throw away, fling; 2. file for metals.
tupatupa, ku-, v.t. huddle.
tupia, ku-, v.t. throw at, to, *nitupie mpira*, throw a ball at me.
tupu, adj. empty, naked, *ni tupu*, it's empty, *yu mtupu*, he is naked.
tura, n. wild tomato, *chuma tura*, pick wild tomatoes.
turubai, ma-, n. canvas.
turufu, n. veto.
tusi, ma-, n. insult, bad remark.
tuta, ma-, n. terraces.
tutika, ku-, v.t. to pile up.
tutumua, ku-, v.t. swell, boast.
tuza, ku-, v.t. award.
twaa, ku-, v.t. pick up, take, carry away..
twanga, ku-, v.t. pound grain.
twanga, ku-, v.t. pound.
twika, ku-, v.t. put a load on somebody's head.
twisha, see **twika**.

U

ua, n. court yard, compound 2. ma-, flower 3. v.t. kill, murder.
uadhimishaji, n. ceremony.
uadilifu, n. chivalry, diligence, integrity.
uadui, n. enmity.
uaguzi, n. divination.
uainisho, n. classification.
uajuzo, n. old age.
ualimu, n. teaching profession.
uamana, n. trusteeship.
uaminifu, n. faithfulness.
uamuzi, n. judgement.
uanamaji, n. seamanship.
uanazuoni, n. scholarship.
uandikaji, n. pen-manship.
uangalifu, n. care, attention.
uangavu, n. transparency.
uasherati, n. promiscuity, lewdness.
uasi, maasi, n. revolt, rebellion.
ubadhirifu, n. extravagence.
ubaguzi, n. discrimination, *ubaguzi wa rangi*, discrimiation based on colour.
ubaharia, n. navigation.
ubahau, n. barbarity, brutality.
ubahili, n. miserliness.
ubalozi, n. embassy, consulate.
ubao, n. board, wood, bench.
ubapa, n. flat surface.
ubaradhuli, n. rudeness.
ubasha, n. sodomy.
ubatili, n. futility.
ubatilifu, n. cancellation.
ubatizo, n. baptism, *siku ya ubatizo wangu*, on the day of my baptism.
ubawa, n. wing.
ubazazi, n. dishonesty, cheating.
ubeberu, n. imperialism.
ubepari, n. capitalism.
ubeti, n. stanza, verse.
ubia, n. partnership in business.
ubikira, n. virginity, *tunza*

ubikira wako, keep your virginity.
ubinadamu, n. humane.
ubinafsi, n. selfishness, egoism.
ubinafsishaji, n. privatisation.
ubingwa, n. skilfulness, expertise, championship.
ubishi, n. dispute, *usifanye ubishi*, don't argue, contention.
ubongo, n. brain.
ubora, n. quality.
ubwabwa, n. cooked rice, also **wali**.
ubwanyenye, n. bourgeoisie.
ubwege, n. foolishness.
ucha, n. reverential fear.
uchachu, n. ferment, sourness.
uchafu, n. dirt.
uchaguzi, n. election, *uchaguzi mkuu*, general election.
uchaji, n. awe, reverential fear.
uchambuzi, n. classification.
uchane, n. bunch of bananas/sugarcane.
uchawi, n. witchcraft.

uchepechepe, n. moisture, dampness.
ucheshi, n. humour.
uchezaji, n. playing.
uchi, n. nakedness, nudity.
uchimvi, n. bad omen.
uchokozi, n. provocation, aggression.
uchongeaji, n. slandering.
uchongezi, n. false accusation.
uchovu, n. fatigue.
uchoyo, n. miserliness, avarice.
uchu, n. longing, passion, strong desire, cupidity, greed, *uchu wa madaraka*, power hungry.
uchukuzi, n. transportation.
uchumba, n. engagement for marriage, courtship.
uchumi, n. economy, *uchumi wa nchi maskini*, the economies of poor countries.
uchungu, n. bitterness, labour pains.
uchunguzi, n. espionage, investigation, research.
uchuro, n. bad omen.
uchuuzi, n. hawking.

udadisi, n. curiosity, espionage.
udaku, n. gossip, iddle-talk, *acha udaku*, stop iddle-talk.
udalali, n. auctioneering, brokage.
udanganyifu, n. cheating, duplicity.
udenda, n. spittle.
udenguaji, n. pomposity.
udevu, ndevu, n. beard.
udhaifu, n. weakness, foible.
udhi, ku-, v.t. annoy, upset, affront.
udhika, ku-, v.i. be upset, angry.
udogo, n. diminution.
udongo, n. earth.
udugu, n. relationship, kinship, affinity, fraternity.
uenezi, n. dissemination.
ufa, nyufa, n. crack; *usipoziba ufa utajenga ukuta*, if you neglect a crack you will have to rebuild a wall (prov.).
ufafanuzi, n. explanation, clarification, *toa ufafanuzi*, give clarification.

ufagio, n. broom.
ufahamu, n. comprehension.
ufanisi, n. efficiency.
ufarisi, n. credential.
ufasaha, n. correctness and clarity of language, fluency, eloquence.
ufashisti, n. fascism.
ufedhuli, n. contempt.
ufidhuli, n. arrogance, ill-will.
ufisadi, n. debauchery, corruption, adultery.
ufito, fito, n. stick, pole for building.
ufizi, n. gum.
ufukwe, n. shoreline, coast.
ufundi, n. skill, craftmanship.
ufunguo, funguo, n. key(s).
ufupi, n. brevity.
ufuta, n. simsim, sesame seeds.
ugaidi, n. terrorism, *fanya ugaidi*, practise terrorism.
ugali, n. stiff porridge.
uganga, n. medical profession, *udaktari*, practice of traditional

and modern medicine.
ugavi, n. distribution, supply.
ugawaji, n. distribution.
ugeni, n. strangeness, special visitor, visitation.
ughaibuni, n. abroad.
ugomvi, n. quarrel, *ugomvi usiofaa,* useless quarrel.
ugoni, n. adultery.
ugonjwa, ma-, n. sickness, disease, *ugonjwa usiotibika,* incurable sickness.
ugua, ku-, v.i. become ill.
ugumba, n. sterility, infertility, barrenness.
ugumu, n. hardness, toughness.
ugunduzi, n. innovation, discovery.
uguza, ku-, v.t. nurse a sick person.
uhaba, n. shortage, scarcity.
uhai, n. life, *maji ni uhai,* water is life.
uhaini, n. treason, *kesi ya uhaini,* treason case.
uhakiki, n. literary criticism.
uhakimu, n. judgeship.
uhalifu, n. crime.
uhamiaji, n. immigration.
uhamisho, n. transfer.
uhanithi, n. impotence.
uharamia, n. piracy, *uharamia wa vitabu,* books piracy.
uharibifu, n. destructiveness, *mharibifu,* destructive person, havoc.
uhariri, n. editorial work.
uharo, n. running stool.
uhasama, n. hatred, animosity, enmity, antagonism.
uhasibu, n. accountancy, *kozi ya uhasibu,* accountancy course.
uhayawani, n. beastliness.
uhitaji, n. imitation.
uhodari, n. bravery, courage.
uhondo, n. sweetness.
uhuni, n. mischief, lawlessness, hooliganism.
uhuru, n. independence.
uhusiano, n. relationship, connection.
uimara, n. firmness, stability.
uingizaji, n. importation.

uislamu   ukarimu

Uislamu, n. Islam.
ujahili, n. cruelity, brutality.
ujalidi, n. bookbinding.
ujamaa, n. brotherhood, socialism.
ujana, n. youthfulness.
ujane, n. widowhood, widowerhood.
ujangili, n. poaching.
ujanja, n. cleverness, craftiness, tricks, *usijaribu ujanja wowote*, don't try any tricks.
ujasiri, n. bravery, audacity, courage, feat.
ujasusi, n. espionage.
ujauzito, n. pregnancy, gestation.
ujazo, n. volume, capacity.
ujenzi, n. building, construction.
ujeuri, n. arrogance.
uji, n. porridge, gruel.
ujima, n. communalism, subsistence economy.
ujinga, n. foolishness, ignorance, folly, *ujinga wa viongozi*, leaders' folly.
ujira, n. wages, salary.
ujirani, n. neighbourliness.
ujoli, n. free slave lineage.

ujumbe, n. errand, *umejia nini*, what is your errand? message, delegation, *ujumbe wa watu sita*, a delegation of six people.
ujumi, n. aesthetics.
ujuzi, n. knowledge, learning.
ukabaila, n. feudalism.
ukabila, n. tribalism, ethnicity.
ukafiri, n. apostasy, sacrilege.
ukaguzi, n. audit, inspection.
ukahaba, n. prostitution.
ukaidi, n. obstinacy, disobedience, stubborness.
ukaimu, n. acting position.
ukakasi, n. acid taste.
ukame, n. drought, aridity.
ukapera, n. bachelorhood.
ukarabati, n. renovation, rehabilitation.
ukarani, n. clerk's office work.
ukarimu, n. generosity, hospitality, *asante kwa ukarimu wako*, thank

ukatili   ukonyoaji

you for your hospitality (kindness).
ukatili, n. cruelty.
ukauleni, n. hypocrisy.
uke, n. vagina, also **kuma**.
ukelele, n. scream, shout.
uketo, n. popcorn.
uke-wenza, n. polygamous marriage.
UKIMWI, n. AIDS, *ameambukizwa UKIMWI*, he is infected with AIDS.
ukindu, n. wild-date-palm leaf.
ukingo, n. edge, rim, bank or a river/lake/ocean.
ukiwa, n. loneliness, forlonness.
ukoka, n. creeping grass.
ukoloni, n. colonialism, *ukoloni mamboleo*, neo-colonialism.
ukoma, n. leprosy, *ukoma unatibika*, leprosy is curable.
ukomea, n. corridor.
ukomo, n. limit, cessation, end, *tumefikia ukomo*, we have come to an end.
ukomunisti, n. communism.
ukongwe, n. decreptitude.

ukonyoaji, n. plucking.
ukoo, koo, n. kinship, lineage, clan, dynasty.
ukora, n. vagrancy.
ukorofi, n. arrogance, trouble making.
ukosefu, n. failure, defficiency, lack of, *ukosefu wa nidhamu*, lack of discipline.
ukosi, n. collar.
ukubalifu, n. consent.
ukubwa, n. greatness, rank.
ukucha, kucha, n. fingernail.
ukuhani, n. priesthood.
ukumbi, n. conference hall, verandah.
ukumbuko, n. memory.
ukumbusho, n. reminder.
ukunga, n. midwifery.
ukungu, n. mist, haze.
ukunjufu, n. cheerfulness, openness.
ukupe, n. exploitation, parasitism.
ukurasa, kurasa, n. page.
ukusanyaji, n. gathering.
ukuta, kuta, n. wall.
ukuu, n. greatness.
ukware, n. nymphomania, lascivous love, hyper-

sexual drive.
ukwasi, n. liquidity, opulence.
ukwato, n. hoof.
ukweli, n. truth.
ulaji, n. consumption, eating.
ulalamishi, n. complaint.
ulanzi, n. bamboo wine.
ulaya, n. Europe, *Ulaya Magharibi*, Western Europe.
ulegevu, n. slackness.
ulemavu, n. disability.
ulevi, n. drunkenness, addiction.
ulimi, ndimi, n. tongue; *ulimi hauna mfupa,* slip of the tongue.
ulimwengu, n. universe.
ulinganifu, n. equation.
ulingano, n. likeness, analogy.
ulingo, n. boxing ring.
ulinzi, n. defence, protection.
uliza, ku-, v.t. ask, enquire.
ulizia, ku-, v.t. enquire into something.
ulokole, n. revivalism.
uma, ku-, v.t. bite 2. cause pain, *kichwa kinauma,* the head is aching.
umaarufu, n. fame.
umahiri, n. ingenuity.
umajimaji, n. dampness.
umalaya, n. prostitution.
umande, n. dew.
umangimeza, n. bureacracy.
umaskini, n. poverty.
umati, n. crowd.
umba, ku-, v.t. create.
umba, n. create, shape, make pottery.
umbali, n. distance.
umbeya, n. tale-bearing, gossip.
umbika, ku-, v.i. be well built, pretty, to be built.
umbile, ma-, n. nature.
umbile, n. nature.
umbua, ku-, v.t. disgrace, expose, contort.
umbuka, ku-, v.i. be disgraced, exposed.
umeme, n. electricity.
umiminikaji, n. pouring.
umiza, ku-, v.t. hurt.
umoja, n. unity.
umri, n. age, *una umri gani?* how old are you?
umwagaji, n. spilling.
unabii, n. prophecy.
unadhifu, n. smartness.

unafiki

unafiki, n. hypocricy, *nachukia unafiki*, I hate hypocricy, *unafiki wa kisiasa*, political hypocricy.
unafuu, n. betterment.
unahodha, n. captaincy.
unda, ku-, v.t. construct, build, design, assemble.
undani, adv. inside, the essence of, interiority,.
undugu, n. kinship, relationship, fraternity.
unene, n. fatness, thickness, obesity.
unga, n. flour 2. join two things 3. ku-, v.t. put spices in food.
ungama, ku-, v.t. confess.
ungamia, ku-, v.t. confess to.
ungamo, ma-, n. confession.
ungana, ku-, v.i. unite, merge.
unganisha, ku- v.t. unite things together, join together.
ungo, n. winnowing basket.
ungua, ku-, v.i. burn, be burned.
unguza, ku-, v.t. set on fire, burn food when cooking.
ununuaji, ununuzi, n. purchasing, buying.
unyafuzi, n. kwashiokor.
unyago, n. rite of initiation done to girls.
unyakuzi, n. snatching.
unyama, n. savagery.
unyang'anyi, n. robbery, *amehukumiwa kwa unyang'anyi*, he has been charged for robbery.
unyarubanja, n. feudalism in the interlacustrine region.
unyayo, n. footprint.
unyenyekevu, n. humility, servility.
unyeti, n. sensitivity, confidentiality.
unyonyaji, n. exploitation.
unyoya, ma-, n. feathers.
unyusi, n. hair of the eye brow.
unywele, nywele, n. hair.
uokovu, n. salvation.
uonevu, n. oppression, spite.
uongo, n. falsehood.
uongozi, n. leadership, *taifa lilineemeka chini ya uongozi wake*, the

nation prospered under his leadership.
uoto, n. vegetation cover.
uovu, n. wickedness.
uozo, n. decay.
upadri, n. priesthood.
upaji, n. endowment.
upakuzi, n. loading.
upambaji, n. decoration.
upambanuzi, n. differentiation.
upande, n. side; *upande ule,* that side.
upatano, ma-, n. concord, harmony.
upele, n. itch, skin erruption.
upelelezi, n. spying, investigation, espionage.
upendano, n. charity.
upendeleo, n. favour.
upeo, n. climax, horizon.
upepo, pepo, n. wind, *pepo mbaya,* evil spirit.
upesi, adv. quickly.
upinde, pinde, n. bow.
upinzani, n. opposition, *vyama vya upinzani,* opposition parties.
upishi, n. cooking.
upole, n. calmness, docility, melancholy.
upoozi, n. decadence.

upotevu, n. wastage, loss of something, *upotevu wa kumbukumbu,* loss of memory, dissipation.
upungufu, n. shortage, deficiency.
upuuzi, n. absurdity.
upuzi, n. nonsense.
upwa, n. niecehood, nephewhood.
upweke, n. loneliness, isolation, forlonness.
upya, n. novelty, newness.
urafiki, n. friendliness, friendship.
urahisi, n. inexpensiveness, cheapness, ease.
uraia, n. citizenship.
urais, n. presidency.
urasimu, n. bureaucracy.
uratibu, n. coordination.
urembo, n. fashion, decoration, beauty.
urithi, n. heritage, inheritance, *urithi wetu,* our inheritance.
uroho, n. gluttony.
urujuani, n. violet.
usafi, n. cleanliness.
usafiri, n. transport.
usafirishaji, n. transportation.

usafishaji   **usiri**

usafishaji, n. cleansing.
usaha, n. pus.
usahibu, n. friendship.
usahihi, n. preciosion, accuracy.
usaili, n. interview, *njoo kwa usaili*, come for interviews.
usajili, n. registration.
usaliti, n. betrayal.
usawa, n. equality, *pigania usawa*, fight for equality.
usemaji-fasaha, n. eloquence.
usemi, n. expression.
usengenyaji, n. backbiting.
useremala, n. carpentry.
ushabiki, n. fanaticism.
ushahidi, n. evidence, *toa ushahidi*, give evidence, testimony.
ushairi, n. poetry.
ushakii, n. demon, courage.
ushanga, n. bead.
ushauri, n. consultancy.
ushemasi, n. deaconship.
ushenzi, n. barbarity, savegery.
ushindani, n. antagonism.
ushindi, n. victory, conquest.
ushirika, n. confederation, co-operative society.
ushirikiano, n. cooperation, alliance.
ushoga, n. friendship between women, 2. gayness, homosexuality.
ushuhuda, n. corroboration, testimony.
ushujaa, n. bravery.
ushungi, n. veil.
ushupavu, n. bravery, firmness.
ushuru, n. customs, *toza ushuru*, collect customs duty; *lipa ushuru*, pay customs duty.
ushuzi, n. farting.
usia, n. will, last word of advice 2. **ku-**, v.t. to give last word of advice, to make a will.
usichana, n. girlhood.
usikivu, usikizi, n. attentiveness.
usiku, n. night 2. adv. at night.
usimamizi, n. supervision.
usinga, n. flywhisk.
usingizi, n. sleep, *shikwa na usingizi*, feel sleepy, fall asleep.
usiri, n. lagging, secrecy, confidentiality.

ustawi — utasa

usitawi, n. prosperity, growth, affluence.
uso, nyuso, n. face(s); *kunja uso*, express sorrow; *uso kwa uso*, face to face.
usoshalisti, n. socialism.
ustadi, n. competence, dexteriy.
ustahimilivu, n. perseverance, patience, endurance.
ustawishaji, n. development.
usufii, n. holiness.
usuhuba, n. friendship.
usukani, n. steering wheel, helm.
usultani, n. sultanship.
usuluhishi, n. mediation, reconciliation, arbitration..
usumbufu, n. bother, disturbance.
usuria, n. concubinage.
utaalamu, n. professionalism, expertise.
utabiri, n. forecast, prophecy, foretell, prophesy.
utafiti, n. investigation, research, *fanya utafiti*, conduct a research.
utaifa, n. nationalism, nationality.
utajiri, n. riches, abundance, richness, wealth.
utakaso, n. purification.
utakatifu, n. holiness.
utalii, n. tourism, *mtalii*, wa-, tourist.
utamaduni, n. culture.
utamadunisho, n. inculturation.
utambo, n. duration.
utamu, n. sweetness.
utanashati, n. neatness, smartness.
utangazaji, n. broadcasting, publicity.
utangulizi, n. preface, foreword, introduction.
utani, n. fun, joke, a relationship in wnich individuals tease one another and are prohibited from taking offense.
utapiamlo, n. malnutrition.
utaratibu, n. arrangement, time-table, schedule, plan.
utasa, n. sterility, barreness.

utashi, n. will, volition.
utata, n. ambiguity, complexity.
utatanisho, n. confusion.
utatu, n. trinity, *utatu mtakatifu*, holy trinity.
utawa, n. monasticism, seclusion.
utawala, n. administration, authority.
utazamaji, n. spectatorship.
ute, n. mucus.
utekelezaji, n. implementation.
utelezi, n. slippery.
utembo, n. fibre.
utendaji, n. exclusion.
utengano, n. separation.
utenguo, n. annulment.
utepe, n. ribbon.
utetezi, n. defence.
uthibitisho, n. confirmaion, verification.
uti, n. backbone.
utii, n. obedience.
utiifu, n. obedience.
utitiri, n. crowd (fleas).
utoto, n. childhood.
utu, n. manhood, *utu wa mtu*, human dignity, being human.
utukufu, n. glory, fame.
utukutu, n. fidget.
utulivu, n. serenity, calmness, composure.
utumbo, n. intestine, *tumbo*, stomach.
utume, n. apostolate.
utumiaji, n. usage.
utumishi, n. service.
utumwa, n. slavery, serfdom.
utundu, n. troublesomeness, mischief.
utungaji, n. composition, writing.
utungisho, n. fertilization.
utungo, n. composition.
utunzaji, n. taking care of, attention.
utupu, n. nakedness, nudity.
uturi, n. aroma, perfume.
uuguzi, n. nursing, taking care of the sick.
uume, n. penis, see also **mboo**.
uungano, n. connection.
uungwana, n. gentility, civility.
uuzaji, n. salesmanship.
uvamizi, n. invasion.

uvimbe, n. swelling, tumour.
uvivu, idleness, laziness.
uvuguvugu, n. lukewarmness, excitement.
uvulana, n. boyhood.
uvumbuaji, n. discovery.
uvumi, n. rumour; *kuna uvumi kwamba...*, it is rumoured that ...
uvumilivu, n. endurance.
uvundo, n. stink, stench.
uvutaji, n. smoking, attraction.
uwajibikaji, n. accountability.
uwakili, n. attorneyship.
uwakilishi, n. representation.
uwalii, n. monasticism, sainthood.
uwanda, n. plain, plateau.
uwanja, n. ground, plot of land, stadium, open space, *Uwanja wa Taifa,* National Stadium.
uwayo, nyayo, n. footstep.
uwazi, n. transparency, openness, vacuum, emptiness.
uwele, n. millet.
uwezo, n. ability, power.

uwiano, n. correlation, ratio.
uwindaji, n. hunting, *kampuni ya uwindaji,* a hunting company.
uwingu, ma-, n. cloud.
uwongo, n. lies, *sema uwongo,* tell lies.
uyoga, n. mushroom.
uza, ku-, v. sell.
uzalendo, n. patriotism, nationalism.
uzalishaji, n. production, *ongeza uzalishaji,* increase production.
uzalishaji, n. production.
uzandiki, n. hypocrisy.
uzao, n. offspring, indigenization.
uzee, n. old age.
uzembe, n. negligence, laziness, carelessness.
uzi, nyuzi, n. thread.
uzima, n. life.
uzinifu, n. adultery, fornication.
uzinzi, n. adultery, debauchery, fornication.
uzio, n. fence, edge.
uzito, n. weight.
uziwi, n. deafness.
uzoefu, n. experience.
uzuri, n. beauty,

mashindano ya uzuri, beauty contest.
uzururaji, n. wandering, loitering, roaming, *anashitakiwa kwa uzururaji*, he/she is accused of loitering.
uzushi, n. false story, rumour mongering.
uzuzu, n. inexperience, foolishness, stupidity.

V

vaa, ku-, v.t. dress up, put on clothes, wear.
vaana, ku-, v.i. embrace in a confrontation.
vali, n. valve.
valia, ku-, v.t. dress well, dress fashionably.
vamia, ku-, v.t. attack, occupy a place without permit, intrude, *vamia nyumba*, break into a house.
vangavanga, n. diddle, garble.
varanda, n. veranda.
vazi, ma-, n. dress, *vazi la kimasai*, maasai dress.
vema, adv. well, good.
vena, n. blood vessel, vein.
veto, n. veto.
via, ku-, v.i. fade away, be stunted.
vibaya, adv. badly.
video, n. video.
vifaa, n. tools, instruments, equipment, *vifaa vya michezo*, sports equipment.
vifijo, n. applause, cheer.
vigumu, adv. hard, with difficulty.
vikapu, n. basketball.
vikorokoro, n. stuff of various kinds, brick-a-brack.
vilevile, adv. also, likewise.
vimba, ku-, v.i. swell.
vimbiwa, ku-, v.i. be constipated.
vingine, adv. others.
vinginevyo, adv. otherwise.
vingirika, ku-, v.i. roll over.
vinjari, ku-, v.i. loitter.
vipi, adv. how? in which way?
viringa, ku-, v.t. roll something into a ball.
visha, ku-, v.t. assit in dressing.
vita, n. war; *pigana vita*, fight a war.
vitamini, n. vitamin.
vitimbi, n. odd actions, unusual behaviour.
vivi hivi, adv. in this same

way, in the same way as.
vivu, adj. lazy.
vivyo hivyo, adv. exactly so.
viza, adj. bad, rotten 2. n. visa.
vizia, ku-, v.t. lay in ambush, ambush.
vizuri, adv. well done.
vocha, n. voucher.
vokali, n. vowel.
volkano, n. volkano.
vono, n. spring bed.
vua, ku-, v.t. undress, *vua nguo*, take off one's clothes, to fish.
vuaza, ku-, v.t. slash.
vugumiza, ku-, v.t. hurl.
vuguvugu, adj. lukewarm. 2. n. movement.
vuja, ku-, v.i. leak.
vuka, ku-, v.t. cross, *vuka mto*, cross a river.
vuli, n. *mvua za vuli*, short rains.
vuma, ku-, v.i. be famous 2. buzz.
vumaika, ku-, v.i. strive.
vumbi, n. dust, *kuna vumbi jingi sana*, there's a lot of dust.
vumbika, ku-, v.t. force fruits to ripe.
vumbua, ku-, v.t. discover, invent.

vumilia, ku-, v.i. endure, bear.
vumisha, ku-, v.t. spread news.
vuna, ku-, v.t. harvest, reap, *vuna mahindi*, harvest maize.
vunda, ku-, v.i. to rot, become rot.
vundevunde, n. mist, fog.
vundo, u-, n. stink, smell.
vunga, ku-, v.i. to cheat.
vungumiza, ku-, v.t. hurl something.
vuruga, ku-, v.t. disturb, mess up, *vuruga akili*, frustrate.
vurugika, ku-, v.i. be in disorder.
vurugu, n. confusion, disorder.
vurumai, see **vurugu**.
vurumisha, ku-, v.t. fling, *vurumisha jiwe*, fling a stone.
vurumiza, ku-, v.t. throw something forcefully.
vusha, ku-, v.t. take across a river, boundary, border etc.
vuta, ku-, v.t. pull, draw 2. attract, entice.
vyema, adv. well and good.

W

wadhifa, nya-, n. rank, position.
wadi, n. ward.
wadia, ku-, v.i. fall due, *siku imewadia*, the day has come.
wahedi, adj. first.
wahi, ku-, v.i. be in time, *wahi kazini*, arrive early at work.
wajibika, ku-, v.i. be responsible.
wajibu, n. duty, responsibility.
wajihi, n. personality, appearance.
waka, ku-, v.i. catch fire, burn.
wakala, n. agency, commission agent.
wakatabahu, pron. yours (in letters).
wakati, nyakati, n. time, period.
wakfu, n. consecration.
wakia, n. ounce.
wakili, ma-, n. advocate.
wakilisha, ku-, v.t. represent.

wala, adv. nor, not.
walakini, n. blemish, fault.
wali, n. cooked rice.
walii, n. holy person, a saint.
wallahi, adv. in God's name.
wamba, ku-, v.t. overlay, strech over, spread.
wando, n. web, *wando wa buibui*, cobweb..
wanga, n. starch 2. ku-, v.i. night activities of witch doctors, ache, pain.
wango, n. computation.
wanguwangu, adv. hastly, fastly.
wanja, n. eye liner.
wanzuki, n. honey local beer.
wao, pron. they .
wapi, wapi 2. adv. in vain, *alijaribu lakini wapi*, he tried but all in vain.
waraka, nyaraka, n. epistle, letter, document of declaration.

waranti

waranti, n. warrant.
waria, n. skilled person.
waridi, n. rose
warsha, n. workshop.
wasaa, n. space, opportunity, chance.
washa, ku-, v.t. ignite, set on fire, irritate.
wasia, n. will, testament, also **wosia**.
wasifu, n. biography.
wasili, ku-, v.i. arrive, reach.
wasiliana, ku-, v.t. communicate with.
wasilisha, ku-, v.t. deliver, hand over.
wasiwasi, n. doubt, anxiety; *tia wasiwasi*, cause anxiety, *ingiwa na wasiwasi*, feel anxious.
wastani, n. average; *kwa wastani*, on the average, mean, approximately.
wavu, nyavu, n. net; *tanda wavu*, set a net.
waya, nyaya, n. wire.
wayawaya, ku-, v.i. sway, stagger.
wayo, nyayo, n. footprint.
wayowayo, n. worry.
waza, ku-, v.i. think, imagine.

wenzi

wazi, adj. clear, open; *mlango uko wazi*, the door is open.
wazia, ku-, v.t. think of, give thought to.
wazimu, n. madness, frenzy.
waziri, ma-, n. minister, *waziri mkuu*, prime minister.
waziwazi, adv. clearly.
wazo, ma-, n. thought, idea.
wazua, ku-, v.i. think deeply.
wee! interj. hey, you!
wehu, n. madness.
weka, ku-, v.i. put, *weka mezani*, put on the table.
wekea, ku-, v.t. put for, *mwekee akiba*, save up for him.
wema, n. goodness, kindness.
wembamba, n. slenderness, slimness.
wembe, nyembe, n. razor blade.
wendo, mw-, n. movement, process.
wengo, n. curved knife.
wengu, n. spleen.
wenzi, mw-, n. friendship,

196

comradeship, friend, comrade.
wepesi, n. alacrity, quickness, lightness, easiness.
werevu, n. cleverness, cunning, shrewdness, intelligence.
weupe, n. whiteness, brightness.
weusi, n. blackness, darkness.
wewe, pers. pron. you, (sing.)
weweseka, ku-, v.i. moving in bed while dreaming.
weza, ku-, v.t. be able to.
wezekana, ku-, v.i. be possible.
wia, ku-, v.t. owe.
wifi, ma-, n. sister-in-law.
wika, ku-, v.i. crow.
wilaya, n. district.
wima, adv. upright, *simama wima*, stand (be) upright, be upright.
wimbi, ma-, n. wave.

wimbo, nyimbo, n. song(s).
winchi, n. winch.
winda, ku-, v.t. hunt, go hunting.
wingi, n. plural, plenty, abundance.
wingu, ma-, n. cloud.
wino, n. ink.
witiri, n. odd number.
wito, n. calling, vocation, casting.
wivu, n. jealousy, *ona wivu*, feel jealous, envy.
wizara, ma-, n. ministry.
wizi, n. theft, robbery.
wodi, n. ward.
woga, n. cowardice, fear.
wokovu, wongofu, n. salvation, *wakati wa wokovu ni huu*, this is the right time for salvation.
wongofu, n. virtuousness, righteousness.
wororo, n. softness, tenderness.

Y

yaani, prep. that is to say.
yabisi, n. dry, hard, parched earth, *baridi yabisi*, a condition of general muscular and skeletal pain resulting from coldness, rheumatism.
yadi, n. yard.
yai, ma-, n. egg, ovum.
yake, poss. pron. his, hers.
yakinifu, adj. true, empirical, scientific, logical.
yaliyomo, n. contents, *angalia kwenye yaliyomo*, look at the table of contents.
yamini, n. oath.
yamkini, adv. probably.
yangeyange, n. white reef heron, *yangeyange nipe kucha nyeupe!*, (literally) white reer heron give me white nails on my fingers!

yao, poss. pron. their, theirs.
yasmini, n. jas-mine flower.
yatima, n. orphan.
yaya, ma-, n. nurse, ayah.
yenu, poss. pron. yours.
yetu, poss. pron. our, ours.
yeye, per. pron. he, she.
yeyuka, ku-, v.i. dissolve.
yeyusha, ku-, v.t. cause to dissolve.
yowe, n. shout, *piga yowe*, shout.
yoyoma, ku-, v.i. go away, disappear.
yumba, ku-, v.i. sway, unstable in direct movement, perform badly in business.
yumkini, see also **yamkini**.
yungiyungi, n. water lily.
yunifomu, n. uniform.

Z

zaa, ku-, v.t. bear offspring, reproduce.
zaana, ku-, v.i. reproduce.
zaba, ku-, v.t. to slap, hit, *zaba kibao*, give somebody a blow.
zabibu, n. grape.
zabuni, ku-, v.i. tender.
zaburi, n. psalm, *imba zaburi*, sing psalms.
zafa, n. procession.
zagaa, ku-, v.i. spread.
zahama, n. hustle, confusion.
zahanati, n. dispensary.
zaidi, adv. more.
zaituni, n. olive.
zaka, n. religious offering, one tenth of one's wealth offered to God as sacrifice.
zalisha, ku-, v.t. produce, be productive, help to give birth.
zama, ku-, v.i. drown.
zamani, adv. formerly, long ago.
zambarau, n. purple.
zamia, ku-, v. to stowaway, to dive, see also **mzamiaji**.
zamu, n. turn, *ni zamu yako*, it is your turn.
zana, n. equipment, tool.
zao, ma-, n. harvest.
zatiti, ku-, v.i. be ready for something (a confrontation).
zawadi, n. gift.
zebaki, n. mercury.
zeeka, ku-, v.i. become old, wear out.
zege, n. concrete.
zembea, ku-, v.i. dally, neglect.
zeruzeru, n. albino.
zeze, n. banjo, fiddle.
zezeta, ma-, n. fool, person with mental problems.
ziada, n. surplus, *zalisha ziada*, produce surplus.
ziara, n. a visit, *fanya ziara*, make a visit, a tour.
ziba, ku-, v.t. fill up a hole, *ziba ufa*, fill up a crack in a wall.

zibua

zibua, ku-, v.t. uncork, unlock.
zidi, ku-, v.i. be more, increase.
zidisha, ku-, v.t. multiply, *zidisha kwa tano*, multiply by five.
zidiwa, ku-, v.t. be overwhelmed.
zigizaga, n. zigzag.
zika, ku-, v.t. bury.
zima, ku-, v.t. extinguish 2. adj. whole, alive.
zimia, ku-, v.i. faint.
zimika, ku-, v.i. go out (fire, light).
zimisha, ku-, v.t. put out (a fire, light).
zinaa, n. adultery, fornication.
zindika, ku-, v.t. protect by charm, *zindika nyumba,* protect house by charm.
zinduka, ku-, v.i. come back to one's senses.
zingatia, ku-, v.t. bear in mind, observe, think of.
zingira, ku-, v.t. encircle, round up.
zini, ku-, v.i. have sex with someone other than one's spouse, practise adultery.

zungukia

zinifu, adj. adulteruos.
zirai, ku-, v.i. faint, lose consciousness, collapse.
ziwa, ma-, n. lake, *Ziwa Viktoria,* Lake Victoria, breast.
zizi, n. stable, shed.
zoa, ku-, v.t. sweep up rubbish.
zoea, ku-, v.t. get used to, *nimezoea hali ya hewa,* I'm used to the weather.
zoeza, ku-, v.t. accustom.
zoezi, ma-, n. exercise, drill(s).
zogo, n. clamour.
zomea, ku-, v. shout insults at.
zuga akili, ku-, v.t. hypnotise.
zuia, ku-, v.t. prevent, encumber, foil.
zuizi, ki-, vi-, n. encumbrance.
zuka, ku-, v.t. appear suddenly, emerge.
zulia, ma-, n. carpet, *zulia jekundu,* the red carpet.
zunguka, ku-, v.i. go round, *zungukazunguka,* wander about.
zungukia, ku-, v.t. go round the other side of.